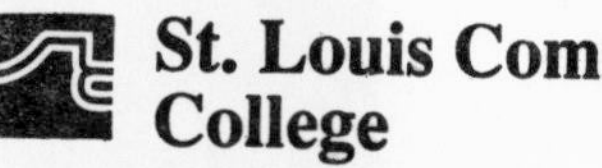

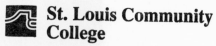

ENTRAILS, HEADS & TAILS

ENTRAILS,

photographic essays
and conversations on the everyday
with ten contemporary artists
compiled and designed
with color photography
by Paola Igliori
with
black and white
photographs
by Alastair Thain

HEADS & TAILS

Louise Bourgeois

James Turrell

Enzo Cucchi

Vito Acconci

Cy Twombly

Gilbert & George

Francesco Clemente

Sigmar Polke

Julian Schnabel

Wolfgang Laib

First published in the United States of America in 1992 by
RIZZOLI INTERNATIONAL PUBLICATIONS, INC.
300 Park Avenue South, New York NY 10010

Library of Congress Cataloging-in-Publication Data

Igliori, Paola.
Entrails, heads, and tails : photographic essays and conversations on the everyday with ten contemporary artists / compiled and designed by Paola Igliori ; with black and white photographs by Alastair Thain.
p. cm.
ISBN 0-8478-1500-5
1. Artists—Interviews. 2. Artists—Portraits. 3. Art, Modern—20th century. I. Title.
N6490.I35 1991
709' .2'2—dc20 91-34990
CIP

Designed and edited by Paola Igliori
Black and white photographs by Alastair Thain
Additional photography by Paola Igliori
Composition design by Paul LeBus

Printed and bound in Hong Kong

Front cover: Photograph by Paola Igliori
Back cover: Collected by Sigmar Polke

To my son Filippo

Introduction

I had thought briefly about having an introduction written by someone else but I realized that this book is about getting away from mediation...it's about experiencing...and the material should speak for itself. Still, I would like to try and say a little more about it. This book is about the everyday and...something else. Uniting the everyday with something that enables us to create it. In a world where everything is analyzed, fragmented, crucified, we seem at times to lose ourselves in the process. Artists, like children, are the most absolute in creating, materializing their own world. The small everyday things that cover the space between the person and his work chart at times in the simplest way the ground of inspiration. This book could be seen as a map that indicates some extreme point of entrance to the core of expression and takes us past it. It is also a discourse on prison and freedom, on how far a human being can go with himself, and on predetermination. Like everything in the universe, it carries within its own key. I started working on this book almost unconsciously—in all my life I had never developed the instruments that most people develop to bridge the chasms within us. There was only a strong unconscious need to explore the going hand-in-hand of death and life, destructiveness and creativity—and where the shift lies. Contraction: our experience of being born repeated throughout our life: fear, aggression, passivity, difficulties. And then expansion: the flow—the ever-reborn second—in which we are one with the action, whole, movement beyond the mind. In plotting the course of an artist's contribution to the world at large, this book hopes to point out how far each of us can go in creating his own world and invites us to tread that same terra incognita.

Paola Igliori

Louise Bourgeois

Le genie n'est que l'enfance retrouvée à volonté l'enfance duée maintenant pour s'exprimer d'organes viriles et d'esprit analytique qui lui permet d'ordonner la somme de materiaux involontairement amassé. C'est à cette curiosité profonde et joyeuse qu'il faut attribuer l'oiel fixe et animalement estatique des enfants devant le NOUVEAU, quel qu'il soit visages ou paysages lumière...

BAUDELAIRE

Genius is nothing other than the capacity to retrieve childhood at will, a childhood now endowed with the ability to express itself through virile organs and an analytic spirit that permits it to organize the sum total of involuntarily amassed data. It is to this profound and joyous curiosity that we must attribute the fixed, animal, ecstatic gaze of children before the NEW, whether in the form of faces, landscapes, light...

BAUDELAIRE

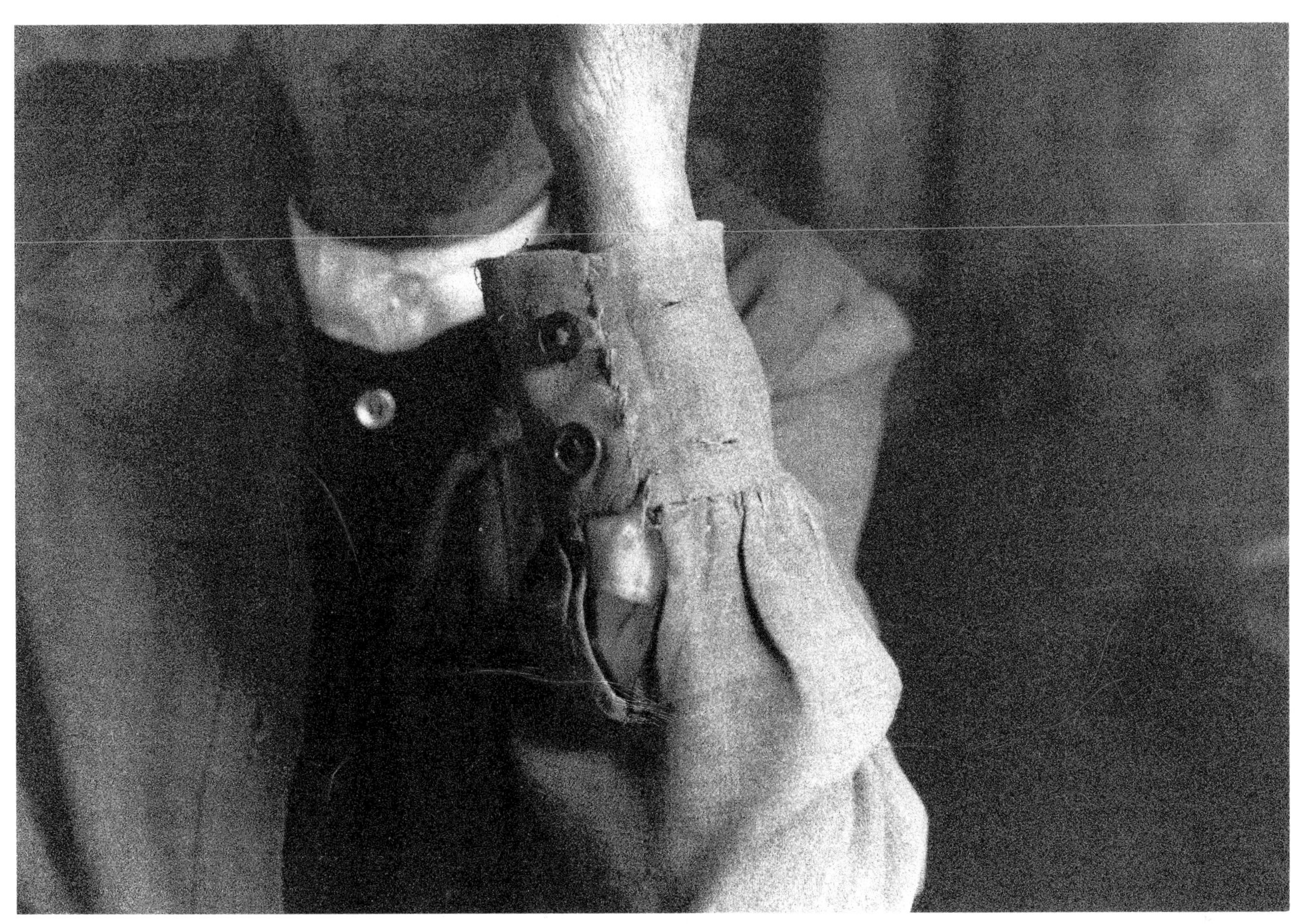

endear yourself
To entertain
in order to divert
a danger
MORNING
BLIND SPOT.
CHEAP LABOR
BLEAK.
late
pretend.
what is your
favorite color?
today
CANNOT cope
Regulate your
insults
So what
Chartres parents scene
Antony escargots scenes
Pietro Elena scene.
get a hold on myself.
to move in on me
or isolate me

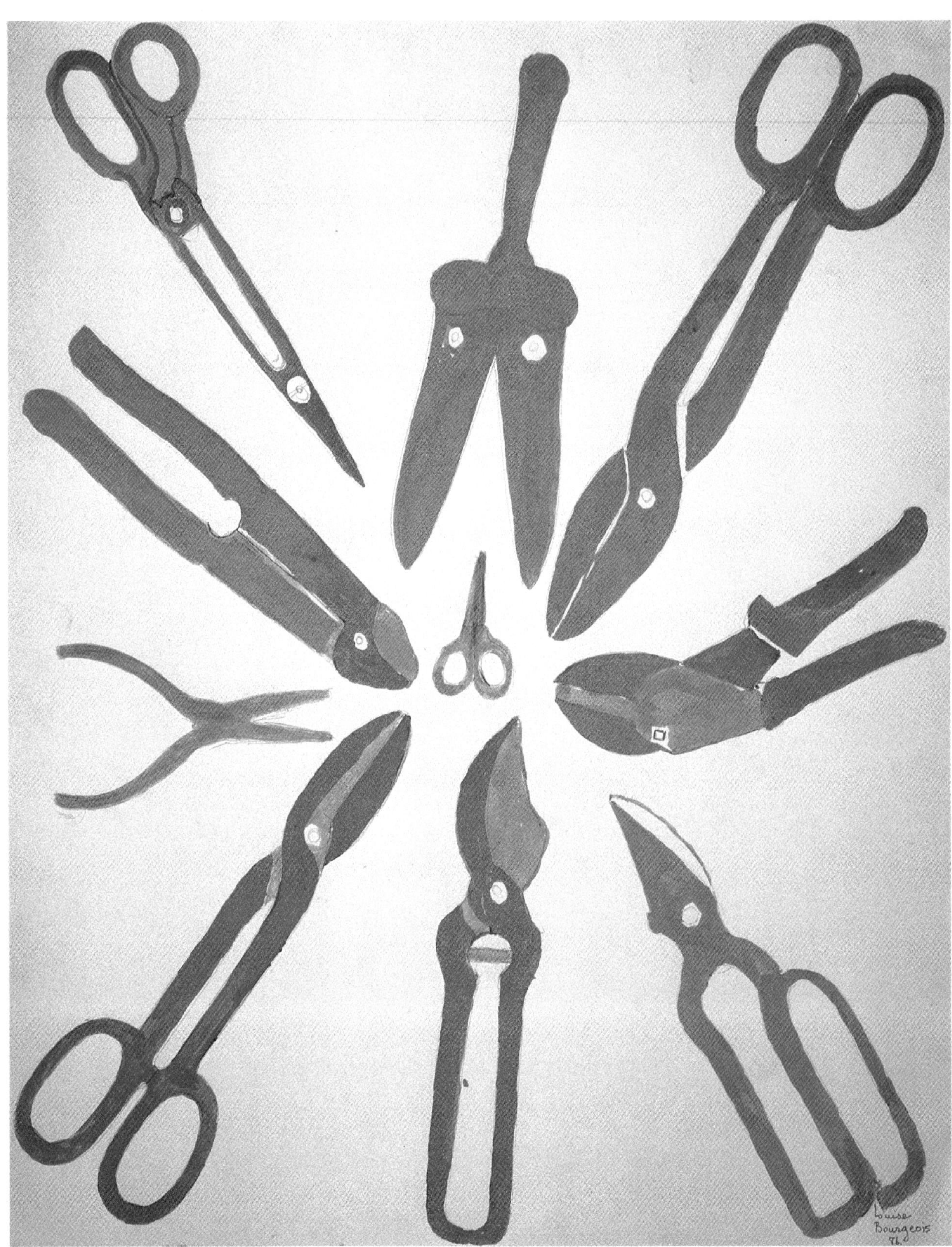
Louise
Bourgeois
86.

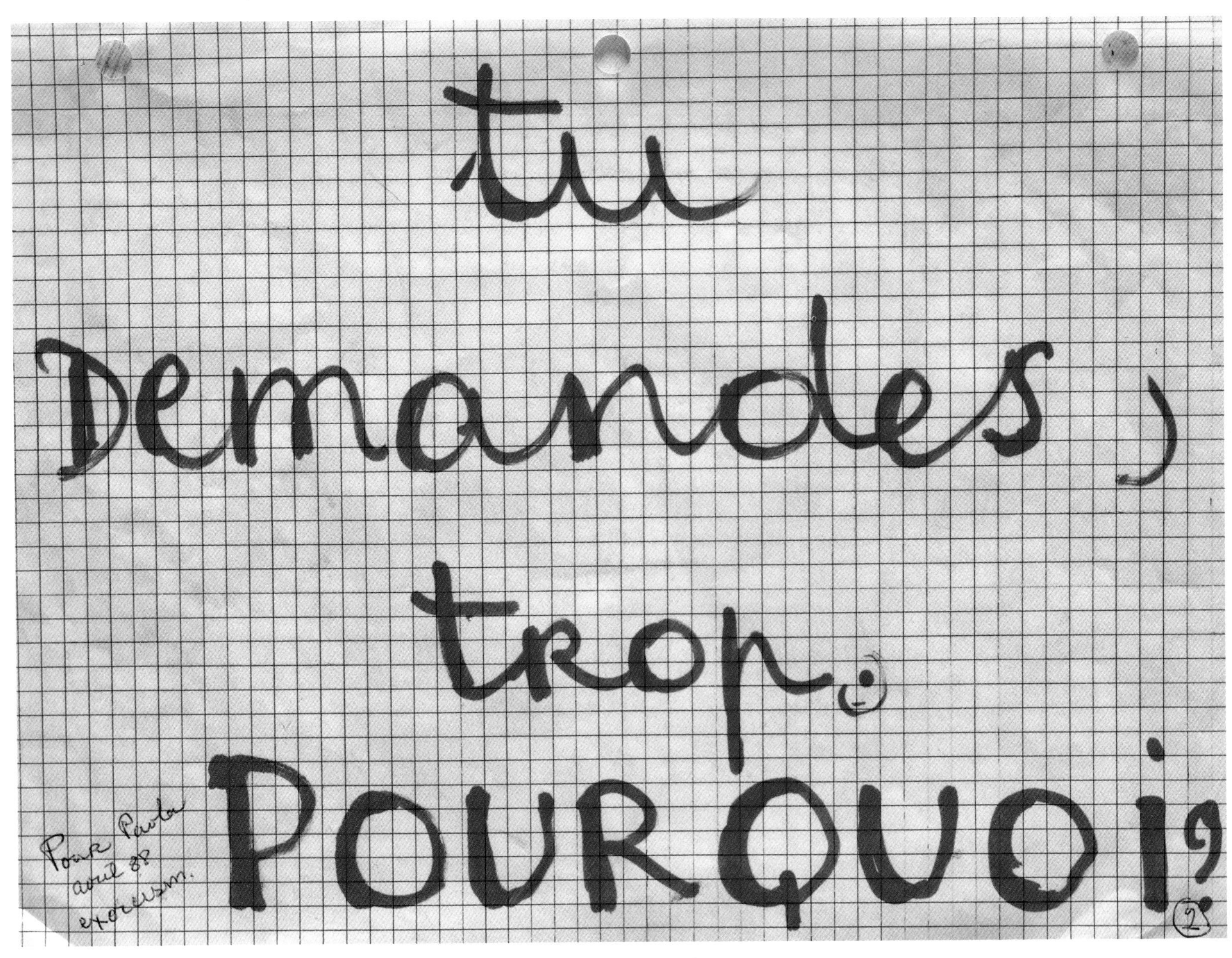
tu
Demandes,
trop.
POURQUOI?
Pour Paula
avril
exorcism.
2

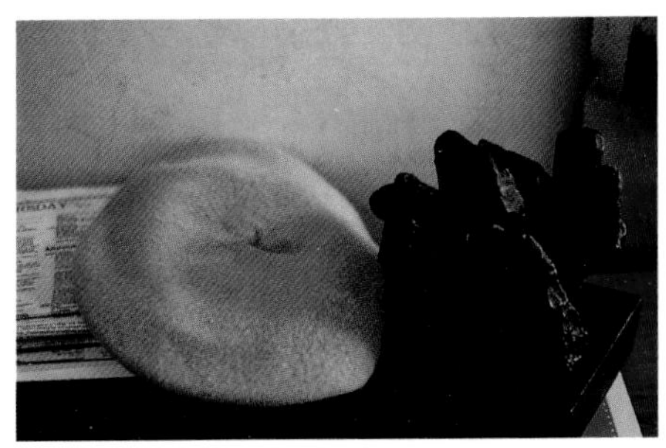

Louise: The house is present from way back. The house is a symbol of togetherness. The house represents five people, the family. So the house represents being at ease and comfortable and safe within this group of five people. When the group was broken up I felt completely helpless and frightened. And that feeling is still present today.

Paola: Your house seems more like a sort of utensil for working and living. You mean the house today? The house today is a studio. And it means that I am free to do whatever I want in it. I have freedom and protection—from harassment, from people making demands. We are in the studio, and the three stone pieces that are finished are going to leave the house, so there has been a great deal of..."harassment" is the word...the harassment of the dust here. The bringing to life of a work of art is a fantastic responsibility—just like children and students are a fantastic responsibility. Why you accept the responsibility I don't know. Because you hope that they will love you for it, but, if this is the hope, it is an error. My son just left for New Mexico and in past years he would leave for Africa and stay for six months or a year, and every time he left I wondered if I would see him again. So it is really a mystery why it affected me so much this time. Maybe this is reflected in the resistance that had to be overcome when I made those stone sculptures. I picked up the challenge of reducing the resistance to nothing; it was a fight to the finish. Now, I think the challenge might likewise be to reconstruct a house, that is to say, a group of five people, when there is no chance in the world that they can be reunited. So it is the drama of something that is falling apart and that you will never be able to put back together again, commonly explained by "Humpty Dumpty Sat On A Wall." And when the egg was broken there was no way to put it back together again. So it is as old as the hills. It is very dangerous to pick up challenges. Maybe only children do that—meaning artists, of course. Who wants to remain a child? Nobody. But the artist remains a child. It is his tragedy. It is not cute at all; it is tragic. But if he grew up, he would never be an artist. You are an artist because you cannot help it. Do you see what that has to do with the house? The destruction

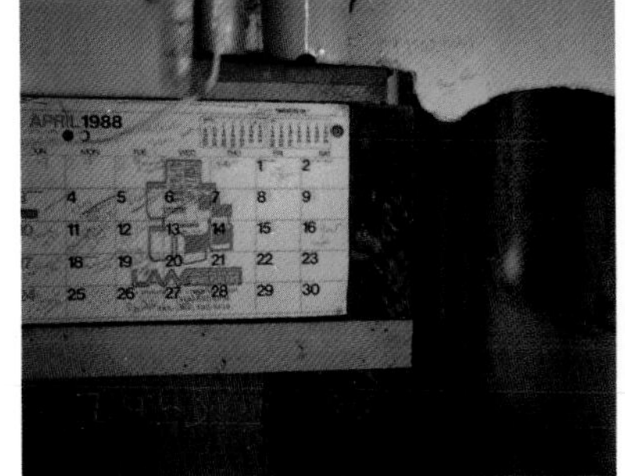

of a house and the attempt at rebuilding a house—in vain? But still trying. Okay, to go back to your question, Paola, about the house. I was talking about the house of childhood, of course, which is so important. But there is another completely different aspect to the house which is the house that the artist lives in, here, now, today, the relationship of running the house and the relationship of life to the realization of the work. It is really the same subject. It is the subject of an environment that is friendly, that you make friendly, and today the house has to be safe and functional. It has to do with the routine of the artist. If the house was not functioning, I could not do the work. It's that simple; the artist is completely dependent on the routine, and the routine is something that you have built yourself, through trial and error, that you improve a little bit day by day and that you trust. The idea of trust is everything. Obviously you could not trust your old house since your old house has abandoned you. No trust is possible there, but the trust in the house is really the trust in the self. You know that. You know that you can depend on the modesty of your ambition, you can depend on your love for cleanliness, for instance. You can depend on yourself. Self-confidence. Self-confidence is necessary for realizing any work. You have confidence in your routine. Your routine is yourself, obviously, if you have made it. And you hope the trust that betrayed you in the past is not going to happen again. So I believe in the routine. To me it is very important. It is sacred, in fact. If the routine was not there, the work could not get done. One is conditioned by the other. The reason is partly that my energy is limited; I don't have too much of it. *What is your routine?* I have habits that I cultivate. For instance, I depend on the trip from the house to the place where I work. Since the person who takes me to the studio works himself from 9 to 5, the trip to the studio has to take place before 9 o'clock in the morning. That is to say, I get up very early, and I work in the mornings. I sort out my ideas and my duties and my plans. The morning hours are my good hours. After that, I have an 11 o'clock slump. Suddenly my world, the outside world, becomes hostile, and I become depressed...and I know what I have to think, and I know what I have to do, and I know what I have to believe at 11 o'clock to get out of the depression. I do not take anything, any chemical of any kind, and I find this strength—you have to have strength to get out of a depression. How do get through the day? Your routine will help you and you help your routine. So it is like a person walking with a stick.

In these stone pieces, there is a large central hole through the middle with many orifices linking the outside with the inside. In effect, in the two or three latest pieces I have made, we are in the presence of a very large cube or rectangle—a block—of stone. What I want to do with the stone is to establish—with my number one tool, which is a level—to establish the center of the stone and to drill right through it, first in a vertical direction, second in a horizontal direction. I want to establish from the start who is the boss. I am the boss of the stone. This is my point. I am not the boss of anything else, but I certainly am the boss of my materials. The material is there to help me and I am not there to enhance the beauty, the polish, or the quirkiness of the material. This is nothing. Crafts people cannot understand my attitude. I want to go to the core of it as if the stone was life itself. I want to ask the question, what is the meaning of this very hard life we have? What is the meaning of suffering? What is the meaning of getting up in the morning for another day's work that will probably be worse than yesterday? What is the meaning of work in life? This is my question, and this is symbolized by this big static piece of stone. As a result, I go right to the question, to the core of the problem (in English you say you get to the core of the problem), by drilling with a bore right through the top—not to the bottom—I don't want to destroy anything. I just want to understand. So the bore goes through approximately the center of the piece in a vertical direction and then, to be sure, to hold the core and not let go of my life's scrutiny, I do the same thing from the side. Because of the tools involved, this is a very strange 20th century attack on the material. The core drill is, let us say, 24 inches across: in my sculpture I use tools that have been made in Italy, among other places, for the drilling of very large holes. They represent the intensity of my scrutiny—scrutiny meaning "what are we doing here?"—which is a philosophical anxiety. I'm not religious so I'm not saying God this, God that; I take my own chances and I take my modest intellectual and artistic means in order to solve the problem. Religion is perfect, but it is not for me. *So what is the light bulb?* The light bulb is a very simple image for, or symbol of, throwing light on a problem. This block of marble represents the problem that we are attacking, namely, what are we doing here? We have only a few more years to live and what have we been doing? What are our children supposed to do? Was it wise or unwise to have children? Those kinds of problems of existence. So the bulb, which is a very simple, symmetrical, reassuring image, is caught in the

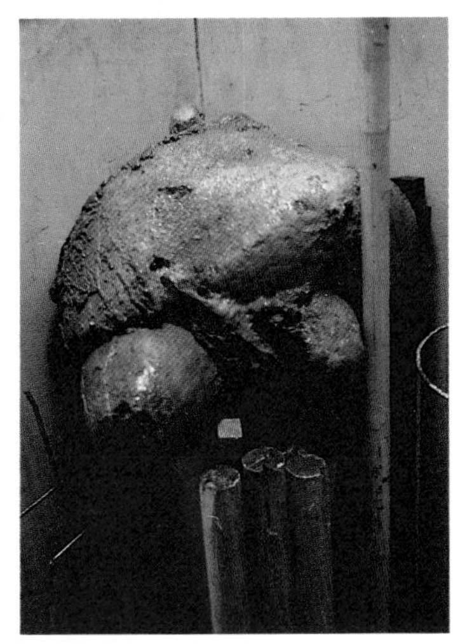

front of this block because I needed a way of getting in, I needed an alley towards the center, and I gave it the shape of a bulb. Why not? In other words, many times the opening is the symbol of scrutiny, which is the eye...But suppose we were blind? I don't think it would make such a difference. If I had been blind, okay, I would have been the same person with the same problems, but obviously the ear, the inner ear, the outer ear would have become terribly important—a means to an end. *An end?* What the motivation is? The motivation is really the desire to practice an exorcism. I practice exorcism in every one of my works. That means that the purpose of the work is to get rid of, or come to a conclusion, or resolve through the scrutiny of a fear. A fear. That's it. To put in order—you can do that through certain crafts. You put a house in order. It is a skill. But to practice exorcism is a skill of a different nature. It is not you who do it; it is your unconscious. And, actually, the unconscious is a beast that you should get rid of because, "interesting" as it is, the unconscious keeps you back. It is the enemy of the new, and what is there in this world except the new? What is there except a new person that you meet? New eyes that you meet? This is the most beautiful thing. To rehash things from the unconscious and suffer like a beast is really repetitive and the sooner you get rid of the unconscious the better. If I don't do any better and if I am held back by the unconscious, it is not through choice; it is really through inability to break through, to break away from problems. You might say, in psychoanalytical terms, that the artist acts out his unconscious instead of resorting to the unconscious and going through new landscapes. And nobody, I'm sorry to say, expressed it better than Baudelaire and especially the young Verlaine. Six horses were holding them back. They didn't like that, they didn't want that, they detested it, and yet they could not break free from it. That is why sometimes I still have hope in sculpture, but I don't have hope in poetry because everything has been said in poetry—everything has been said in words. Sculpture uses language without words, which is deeper. Of course very few people read it, but still it goes one step further. I was reading Pasolini lately, and it was fantastic. We were talking about exorcism. He tried to exorcise the mother figure, that is, the mother figure who is first the great betrayer, the great traitor, and then, much later, he forgives, and he asks for forgiveness from the father. It is absolutely moving as the subject of pain. That's the business I'm in. I'm not very good at forgiving. I would rather forget, but the people that forget actually do not forget. They pretend that they forget, which I think is my case. I pretend, you see. I pretend honestly that I have forgotten France; however, I do not go back because maybe I do not deserve it. I do not deserve to forgive. I do not deserve to be forgiven. I ask for forgiveness through works of art. *What did New York mean to you, coming to America, leaving France?* I turned a page. It is so wonderful to turn a page. *Louise, were there some people who were important to you in your early life in the States?* Coming over on the boat, in 1939, I met Amédée Ozenfant and Marcel Duchamp. They had a certain importance at the time. It meant at least I could speak French to somebody. But it had another importance insofar as these people have remained in history—for instance, the history of the McCarthy trials. *During the McCarthy period you were called to testify but were acquitted. Why did they call you up?* Three French people who did not have their American citizenship were called to answer a million questions—Marcel Duchamp, Amédée Ozenfant and Louise Bourgeois. *Who was Amédée Ozenfant?* He was a close friend and a neighbor, a collaborator of Le Corbusier's, and he was an artist and a great teacher. He had a school in Paris and also on 20th Street here in New York. We three were investigated separately; part of this was questioning by the F.B.I. It was not difficult for me to say I was not a communist, even though I had gone to Russia twice, as a student. *Was this a problem, that you had been to Russia?* No. Just because you go to Russia, you don't approve of everything that they do. I am more interested in the differences between theories, people, materials than in common denominators. So to go to Russia as a student was a must for my education. This I explained to them...and they understood it. There were no charges. It was simply an investigation. My husband was involved politically. I could not be made responsible for his opinions, and he was very strong about this, so I was released—released as innocent. I don't know very well of what—but innocent. This was history. Marcel Duchamp got off the hook because of the influential friends he had in government, including Pierre Matisse. It reminds me of the period during the war—what was the relationship of Pierre Matisse to the French government, of Marcel Duchamp to the administration? Mr. Ozenfant was not able to defend himself. This was such a pain for him that he went to the south of France, to a hotel room, and died. It was an emotional, wrenching experience. *What did you do when you first came to the States?* The first thing I did was to reassure my husband that I would not be a charge for him and that I had my own interests—one of the reasons he married me, among many others which I never understood. His mother had not been independent, but she had harassed the entire family with her feminist stance, and he wanted to marry a girl who would be self-sufficient, if not emotionally, at least professionally. So in order to reassure him I registered at the Art Students League the next day after I arrived in this country, to show him that if I took these courses he could be working at home alone while I was at school—a very strange attitude, but it suited him very well and it suited me perfectly well, too. You must understand that I was very young, and I had no expectation of being known. My first show took place almost ten years after I touched this shore. I was not at all one of the exiled artists, like Duchamp, Masson. I was a whole generation younger than any of them, which people don't even realize today. You asked me who was important to me. My motivation was built on antagonism against the past. I was rather an iconoclast. The fact that the exiles were important is true, but they were important because they gave me a target to revolt against. What challenges me is the resistance that problems offer me. Somebody said about me, "Louise likes a fight." It is not that I like a fight; it's that when I fight I feel alive. Do you understand? *Yes, and it shows a lot in the materials you use.* I am working for somebody...but I am working against the material. For me, a significant image of motivation is the *Jongleur de Nôtre Dame* in *Les Miserables*. The *jongleur* is a poor devil completely alone in the world. He is an artist, no more or less, just an ordinary artist, and he can work only if he can work for somebody—as a child works for the teacher, whether the teacher sees him or not. The *jongleur* has decided that he would give his life for *Nôtre Dame,* the Virgin, if only she would notice that he was alive. So he works, poor devil. He works for years to accomplish his foolishness, juggling in the air, and finally he gets to be very good and once he puts his life on the line in front of her. Believe it or not, she cracks a smile! He had accomplished what he wanted. So I am this juggler, really. *Everything makes me think of being in the inside of things with you—from the way you live in your house to the way you go to your studio across the river, by subway. And in your work, even if now you have some more specific images, the main body of it seems to be tackled from the inside. This is a very female thing, feelings that can be touched.* That was not a question—it was a statement. But I see the question behind the statement. May I answer your question by referring to a work of art? Let's refer to the Whitney piece. It's called *Cleavage.* You know I have six or seven titles for every piece because I forget them. It is a stone which is seven feet or more long, right? About four feet deep and four feet high—very large. Nobody, but nobody, said a single word about it because it was strange. It *is* strange. It is difficult to know what I mean about it, but I can tell you. The deep gut feeling that you are referring to in your question is translated here by the imprint of my leg. You see? The knee is there. And here are the two legs of my love interest at the time. Right? So that is a terribly deep feeling. *It represents a need?* The need to give reality to maybe an impossible need, an impossible hope, an impossible emotion, by imprinting it in stone. It cannot be simpler; the term "feeling" is not strong enough. "Emotion" would be more appropriate. The word to mention now is "frustration." Why should you work so hard trying to understand something if it was not motivated and fueled by frustration? That's it. Or terror, or something that you simply cannot endure, emotions that are so painful you are going to scream. Well, that's what people do all the time. They scream and they scream, and

yet it doesn't affect their pain, whereas the artist, who is a privileged character—nobody knows that—has the privilege to give meaning and shape to his suffering. That's why we accept the suffering. Otherwise, we would kill ourselves ten times a day. Of course you want to talk about the house and the habits and the nature of the routine and then *why* your routine's different from my routine, which is very valid, very interesting. But my interest, that is to say, the subject that makes me feel ignorant, and that I am never tired of, is the mechanism, the psychological mechanism, of the self-destructiveness of the artist. I said before that the artist is a privileged character, he's a nut. But if you are big enough to accept your privilege, then the fight begins and the work begins. My work is to try to understand what makes the artist a self-defeating creature. Is it because the artist is guilty about knowing, inside, never admitting it, that he's a privileged character? I think this is it. We are trying to say that we suffer like beasts and we are do-gooders. Actually we are not; we are exactly the opposite. We are ashamed and guilty. Of course the guilt and the shame is completely different, but it has to be explored. We're ashamed and guilty of having that gift. The gift of total recall, which is very, very useful, and which is a gift of the gods, is given to very few people. Sometimes you find these creatures in the street or at a party who are natural—some people are natural artists, natural actors, or natural storytellers. Well I hate storytellers. Let me tell you I cannot stand them. This is really beside the point. The fact remains that the storytellers have a gift. It is a gift that was very, very highly rewarded and paid for in the old days. Now storytellers are not much in demand because they are imitated. But when you find a real storyteller—I don't know where you can find them, probably in hospitals—they have a magic. In fact, they're entertainers...you see, I am the daughter of a storyteller. This is why I can dismember them, put them back together again and see their flaws. I want to be more than a storyteller. Do you understand? In fact, I want self-expression, and storytellers fool people all the time. That's why we love them, but they're really clowns. A storyteller is somebody who is not honest with himself or herself, and I want to go much deeper than that. That's my ambition. *Dismembering, that brings me to what I'd been meaning to ask you about the body.* When I'm listening to you, I associate in my mind. As the word "frustration" came to my mind just before, for storytelling, now the word "articulation" appears. That is to say, the word emotion is translated into a bodily happening, a bodily phenomenon which takes the shape "articulation." Suddenly I move my leg, or suddenly I move my arm, suddenly I move my thumbs, so we are in the physical, we are in the body's languages now. The stone becomes the body. Self-expression—instead of moving my arm, my shoulder blade, which is not terribly interesting or unique—becomes unique through a translation in the body. What happens to my body is repeated in the stone, except that then it has to add a formal meaning. It has to relate and be expressed in a different world. The world of words is not my world. My world is the material, not particularly stone. It could be clay. But my body becomes material—and I express what I feel through it; and if I'm lucky—or is that the essence of talent?—I make it communicate to you. *And often the body is dismembered.* Well, the body is always dismembered, of course, what a child does to a toy. You try to destroy but you don't. For instance, if my mother did not do immediately what I wanted, I had images of twisting her legs, killing her. This is the subject of the work called the *She-wolf,* whereby I would kill my mother every time she refused me something. But, by the same token, five minutes later I said, "Louise, you shouldn't have done that; now you better rebuild it because she might get angry at you." So before she got angry at me, I rebuilt her. It is a constant shifting from destroying to the phoenix. *Death is also present in your work in this dismembering. Is it done to reach a further stage, another putting together?* The child experiences that, and the artist in a state of inspiration suddenly goes back to that omnipotence of the child and exerts it on the material. Simple as that. *You said earlier, "Why all this pain, all this hard work?"* Well, the pain is the ransom of your ignorance. The reason is that we are inadequate. We suffer because we do not know any better. You have the horrible pain of a cat touching a stove, or a child, or yourself touching a stove and getting a horrible burn. Well, you certainly cannot deny the pain of the burn, but it's your fault. If you realized in your bones what a stove is, that is, danger, and what your body is, that is to say, unable to stand a burn, you would not suffer. You wouldn't experience pain if you knew better. It's just that you are inadequate and you try to put the blame on someone else. You got burned because you didn't know any better. Children should be protected from the neuroses of their parents. That is a fact. I suffer myself from the little neurotic traits of my father and mother. It's ridiculous what I say, but our birthright should be to be born in a sophisticated and loving family. Along with self-expression, it is one of our birthrights. Otherwise we spend a lifetime recovering from the terrible abuse—abuse is a bad word—but from the terrible self-indulgence of our parents. To atone for, to pay for what? For the suffering of someone else. That's what I mean by the ransom. *I envy people who don't experience this torture and who just flow and take the little things in life in stride.* That you would like to be happier is obvious. *Maybe all this pain enables one to get in touch with some deeper level; it's there for something.* This is a religious attitude; the religious attitude is that if you find a stone in your garden that bothers you, and it keeps you from planting something, you keep it because you feel it must have a purpose. I don't believe in that; I believe we have to take our

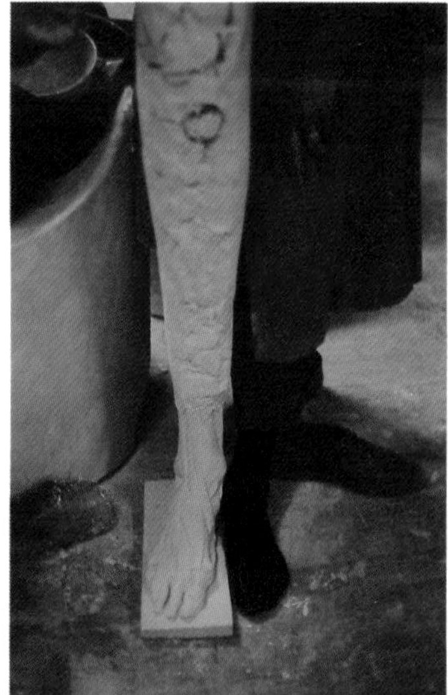

own chances. What helps when we try to be precise and better at self-expression? I don't know what helps you, but a lump of sugar will do it for me, will give me the means not to panic, to stay on an even keel. Of course, it has its ransom, you know. That is to say, it helps you in case of panic, but you pay for it by having to get another lump of sugar on the next occasion; you see, it creates a need. Looking at somebody else's eyes works too, but sometimes it's impossible. *Did you always manage to keep this routine so connected with work when you were working at home and you had your family?* Absolutely... Always. *Was it hard with the children?* I felt sometimes I wasn't a good enough mother; but I never wanted that devastating influence parents can have on children. I always had to tell them from early on that mother and father are not gods, but just poor devils who try to do the best they can. *You told me that when your husband died you removed the stove from the kitchen to somewhere in the basement, but you cooked regularly.* It meant a lot, it meant pleasing the family, but you know I think that cooking is a way of hiding things from each other. For instance, people have a so-called "good time" and they eat a lot and they drink a lot and actually they manage to stay on the surface of things. Nothing is ever said. Food allows us to talk about trivia, and be pleasant without asking the real questions of life. So to have good food with people is a way of drowning the fish. *What do you think about interviews?* Interviews? I feel very strongly about interviewers. I feel that they put me in a state of anxiety most of the time, but I have studied the anxiety and have discovered that there is a chemistry between the interviewer and the interviewee, and I did not know it until now. I feel that I do very well, from my point of view, with certain people, and I am absolutely disastrous in other situations. And people make me say things that manipulate me against my will. And it's a catastrophe. But I don't have to despair because I have been able to be interviewed by people who make sense to me and make sense out of me and do not frighten me to a crisp, allow me to be my little self. *Do you have any theories on how and why your relationships exist and grow?* If I take the realized works as a frame of reference for this question, I would say that the entrances and exits in all my "lairs" and environments are direct representations of relationships. It has to do with the polarity between finding and

calculating a relationship versus the absolute terror of responsibility and desire to escape a trap. That is to say the polarities between control, fear of losing control, and the admission that there is no question of control, you have none. When you feel "high" you feel you have some control and you feel very jealous of this control. When you are in a negative frame of mind you accept the fact that you are manipulated against your will, but what can you do? You need a lot of strength and a lot of faith. When you are pessimistic you become prey to your fear and run away. It goes back and forth between two poles. And it explains the polarities in most of my work—pleasurable and with danger, one unrealistic and the other safe and depressive in tone. The entrances and exits are an effort to avoid the trap. *In your studio in Brooklyn you actually have in the smaller rooms real double entrances and exits. I saw at least four; even the bathroom has a double entrance.* Yes, absolutely. It is very important to me. The entrances and exits are an effort to avoid the trap. They cannot trap me because I am running as fast as I can. (both laugh.) I move in and out of relationships; I do not stay in relationships because they frighten me. *One day you asked me what kind of friends I attracted. You told me you needed people who were always very rational. The friends you attracted seemed to be mistreated by their parents, the women mainly. What I am looking for has more to do with the relationships you may have with your friends. Do you have a theory of why relationships grow, why people are attracted to each other?* This is rather simple. When I am outgoing or an optimist, I want a relationship with somebody older, who will boss me around and save me; I want to be rescued; I am a damsel in distress. This is the optimist part of myself. When I am depressed I need to fold up, to find cover, and to find a mother, so the polarities are very clear. Does this relate to the question? I am attracted to my own selfish pleasure, I am attracted to men who are going to save me from distress! This is a complete dream, still, I want it even though I know it is absurd. I am flattered by people who want my affection and my love, so the polarity is do you want to love or do you want to be loved? Well, it is obvious; I don't have to answer that question. I have never found a relationship where the two were present, 50/50. I love you 50% of the way. In other words I have never found a relationship that was equal. To find each other half-way is just perfect. But to provide 75% of the energy in a relationship you have to be very rich in energy and you

cannot always afford that much giving. But when people are older than I am, they can give me, if not guidance, reassurance. People who are strong enough, energetic enough, give me some rules that they are not going to break, even if *I* break them. They give me confidence in their morality, but very specially in their ability, their capacity. This is not a matter of wanting but being able to, what one is able to provide. Are you able to take care of a relationship, able to take care of an event when you are possessive? When you see a betrayal in your friend, are you able to solve it or integrate the betrayal of the other one? I am not able to. That is for sure. But I expect other people to forgive me. So that is my erotic situation; I am really a *femme infant.* And I can admit that. I have never been able to find someone strong enough to see me as a *femme infant;* people see me as a mother. I'm not a mother; I'm a baby! It's absurd. The whole thing is absurd. *The other day, suddenly, you asked me, "Do you think Andy Warhol was a virgin when he died?"* Well, he was a homosexual, so he was not a virgin. *There are a lot of sexual references in your work that I do not see as "sex" references, but more power references. In a way I see you as a shy girl...* My intention is never to be erotic; if people see it as erotic it is their input. What I want is to be different; my possessiveness is that I want to be myself. My work is self-expression. What is self-expression? When people ask me, I say I really don't know and I really don't care. This is my privilege; it is my birthright, and I don't know where it came from. It does not make any difference to me; why should it make any difference to you? You react to the work and like it or else it is just too bad. Don't ask me why I did it; I just wanted to. I do not want to give any account to anybody. When people talk about communication—collaboration, cooperation—all this is so condescending! This is not my kind of world. I couldn't care less about communication. The terrible thing about self-expression is that it's not an end in itself: to express myself does not make me grow. This is why I never grew up. No one ever gave me a chance; they spoiled me. I grew into sublimation. But even self-expression within sublimation is not an end; it's not an experience. The definition of experience is that, after the experience, you are a different person. You have grown up. When you choose sublimation, you do not grow up. It is an acting out, and it is not a progress. If I am a bad girl because of that, well, so what! I don't pretend to communicate; this is the point. I would like to...but it is not up to me. *Will you show me the studio downstairs and the garden? Do you still work here sometimes?* A certain amount of work is done here. The small pieces which have to be joined together, or drilled

together, I do here, so I have a lot of tools here. A thief saw these tools from the basement window and broke in. He was leaving with the lot of them, but a neighbor called the police. You have to be nice to your neighbors here, not because you're good—I'm not pious—but you need your neighbors and the neighbors need you sometimes. It's the artist in society, how they are accepted—if they're useful, if they are a pain in the neck. What is the idea of the artist in a community? Here no one knows that I am an artist. They know me as a person who will clean up, who helps the neighborhood, or who is injurious to the neighborhood. It's not fast friendship: you tolerate the neighbors because they tolerate you. *In the garden, all the branches of the trees have been shaped into loops.* These are little portraits of my friends. It is a very small place so the trees have to go up, otherwise the plants do not have enough sun and air. So everything is trimmed at the bottom, like in a forest. Instead of cutting the trees, I turn them into loops, and I make them into the figure "8," or I turn them into spirals. *So here also the material has to do what you want.* Yes, but you see I do not cut it. I do not destroy it. I kind of use it. And it works very well. But this is called topiary. *There are a few kettles next to the sink in the kitchen.* I'm not a compulsive collector like Warhol, but I collect gifts. For example, what I really like to have in the house is kettles; one can't have a house without a kettle.

Sometimes I find wonderful kettles like this one here with a copper bottom—*formidable*—so I collect them. I'm boiling some water for the pasta in this big one. *You boil water for the pasta in the kettle?* Always, it's faster—it whistles when it's ready. One doesn't forget about it and go out into the street. Look at this one, wonderful quality! I buy them because I can't resist them. And I tell myself I can buy them because I have a gift to make. Then I don't dare offer the gift—I don't dare say, "Would you like a kettle?"—because I'm afraid of the rejection.

At your studio I've seen collections of useful objects; there were two shelves full of all sorts of clamps, coming from different utensils. One always needs clamps; they are absolutely

indispensable. You clamp wood together...They have all sorts of uses. *You have also made some pieces with various cutting utensils.* Oh, yes. That is a plate of cutting instruments. It has to do with revenge; it has to do with cutting somebody who has hurt you. *The opposite of that marble piece you did with breasts carved out from a marble tree stump.* That is a carving of a breast and of a protective part of the body cut out of a solid block of stone. You may say that this is the opposite of the plate of tools. One nurturing and the other is destroying; these are different aspects of the same person. *What are these lead plates on the floor?* There are round plates of lead everywhere. There are lots of wires on the floor. If you didn't have the plates you would always trip. *There is a room with a bed and all sorts of linen piled up and folded on it.* That is the linen room: *la lingerie.* A linen room is essential, very necessary for the routine. Here I dry the clothes. *From la lingerie there is a tiny door, just your size, to a bathroom, with a lot of clothes hanging in rows over the bathtub.* There is a cross-ventilation system; if I keep the back and front windows of this flat open, the clothes dry hanging. It is very important, because it is so neat. If you had this outside everything would be dirty immediately. *So even this has to do with self-sufficiency?* But you must understand very well, coming from Italy. Everybody in Italy and France, in the middle class, has help. I

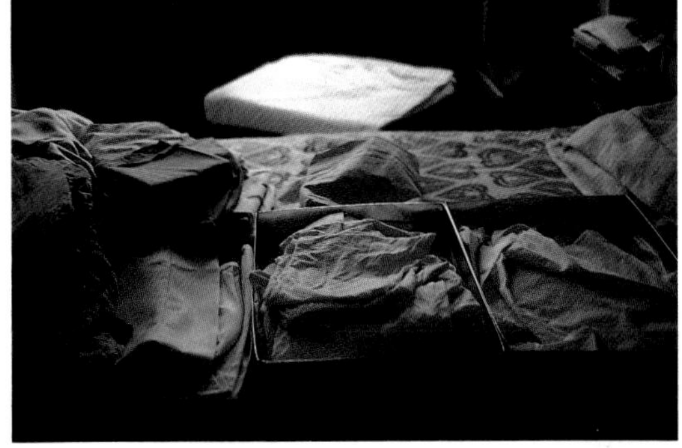

came from that special group. When I was in school they called me "Mademoiselle Lison." They would say to my father, "Mademoiselle Lison wants to go to school." And, when you get here to the States, there is absolutely nobody to help; you have to do your own work. When I had my three children I had no help in the house. There was an incredible amount of work. *In the cellar, large meters and wires are showing and ticking high up on the wall.* But this is very modern. What is special about this is that it is very modern, very neat, you know. All these meters are suspended for protection because the water comes and floods the basement. *The floor is incredible. It seems to be taken out of the bed of a river.* Yes, exactly. The river used to flood very often and this is the original floor. New York used to be called New Amsterdam. Everything is original and untouched in this house; it's the last house like this on the street. This is the coal chute here. But then these meters and the furnace are very modern. This is the old furnace, abandoned—everything is abandoned every five years in America. *This house is like a whole world, in a way. There's a cellar with stone from the river...* A tiny world.... *Yes, I love the doors cut to your size.*

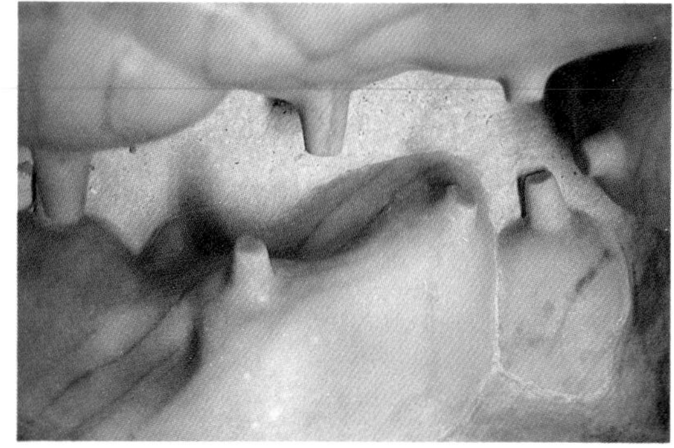

The studio in Brooklyn is cement, you know, very modern. This, instead, is very old and it is untouched. In the back of this you have the fireplace. There are six fireplaces here. *What is this green hose for?* It's to clean the dog's caca on the sidewalk. You just reach right out of the window with it—here! (showing) And I do it for other people. I'm a very good neighbor. It is not that I'm a very good neighbor, but I try to be. I feel that you have to be a good neighbor. I clean for the whole neighborhood.

James Turrell

JOHN C. VAN DYKE, <u>THE DESERT</u>, SCRIBNE
NEW YORK, 1901.

1

P. 1

IT IS THE LAST CONSIDERABLE GROUP OF MOUNTAINS BETWEEN THE DIVIDE AND THE LOW BASIN OF THE COLORADO DESERT. FOR DAYS I HAVE BEEN WATCHING THEM CHANGE COLOR AT SUNSET — WATCHING THE CANYON SHIFT INTO GREAT SLASHES OF BLUE AND PURPLE SHADOW, AND THE RIDGES FLAME WITH EDGINGS OF GLITTERING FIRE.

I RIDE AWAY THROUGH THE THIN MESQUITE AND THE LITTLE ADOBE RANCH HOUSE IS SOON LOST TO VIEW. THE MORNING IS STILL AND PERFECTLY CLEAR. THE STARS HAVE GONE OUT, THE MOON IS LOOKING PALE, THE DEEP BLUE IS WARMING, THE SKY IS LIGHTENING WITH THE COMING DAY. HOW COOL AND CRYSTALLINE THE AIR! IN A FEW HOURS THE GREAT PLAIN WILL BE ALMOST LIKE A FIERY FURNACE UNDER THE RAYS OF THE SUMMER SUN, BUT NOW IT IS CHILLY. AND IN A FEW HOURS THERE WILL

2

SET WAVERING ACROSS THE WASTE UPON THE OPALESCENT WINGS OF THE MIRAGE. BUT NOW THE AIR IS SO CLEAR THAT ONE CAN SEE THE BREAKS IN THE ROCKY FACE OF THE MOUNTAIN RANGE, THOUGH IT IS FULLY TWENTY MILES AWAY. IT MAY BE FURTHER. WHO OF THE DESERT HAS NOT SPENT HIS DAY RIDING AT A MOUNTAIN AND NEVER EVEN REACHING ITS BASE? THIS A LAND OF ILLUSIONS AND THIN AIR. THE VISION IS SO CLEARED AT TIMES THAT THE TRUTH ITSELF IS DECEPTIVE.

IN THE DRAWS AND FLAT PLACES THE FINE SAND LIES THICKER, IS TOSSED IN WAVE FORMS BY THE WIND, AND BANKED HIGH AGAINST CLUMPS OF CHOLLA OR PRICKLY PEAR. IN THE WASH-OUTS AND OVER THE CUT BANKS OF THE ARROYOS IT IS SOMETIMES HEAPED IN MOUNDS AND CRESTS LIKE DRIVEN SNOW. IT BLOWS HERE,

3

ALONG THE BOUNDARY LINE BETWEEN ARIZONA AND SONORA ALMOST EVERY DAY; AND THE TAILING OF THE SANDS BEHIND THE BUSHES SHOWS THAT THE PREVAILING WINDS ARE FROM THE GULF REGION. A COOL WIND? YES, BUT ONLY BY COMPARISON WITH THE NORTH WIND. WHEN YOU FEEL IT ON YOUR FACE YOU MAY THINK IT THE BREATH OF SOME DISTANT VOLCANO.

P. 25-26:

ALL THE GENTLER QUALITIES OF NATURE THAT MINOR POETS LOVE TO JUGGLE WITH — ARE MISSING ON THE DESERT. IT IS STERN, HARSH, AND AT FIRST REPELLENT. BUT WHAT TONGUE SHALL TELL THE MAJESTY OF IT, THE ETERNAL STRENGTH OF IT, THE POETRY OF ITS WIDE-SPREAD CHAOS, THE SUBLIMITY OF ITS LONELY DESOLATION! AND WHO SHALL PAINT THE SPLENDOR OF ITS LIGHT; AND FROM THE RISING UP OF THE SUN TO THE GOING DOWN OF THE MOON MOON OVER THE IRON MOUNTAINS, THE

4

GLORY OF ITS WONDROUS COLORING! IT IS A GAUNT LAND OF SPLINTERED PEAKS, TORN VALLEYS, AND HOT SKIES. AND AT EVERY STEP THERE IS THE SUGGESTION OF THE FIERCE, THE DEFIANT, THE DEFENSIVE. EVERYTHING WITHIN ITS BORDERS SEEMS FIGHTING TO MAINTAIN ITSELF AGAINST DESTROYING FORCES. THERE IS A WAR OF ELEMENTS AND A STRUGGLE FOR EXISTENCE GOING ON HERE THAT FOR FEROCITY IS UNPARALLELED ELSEWHERE IN NATURE.

IS THEN THIS GREAT EXPANSE OF SAND AND ROCK THE BEGINNING OF THE END? IS THAT THE WAY OUR GLOBE SHALL PERISH?

NOT IN THE SPOTS OF EARTH WHERE PLENTY BREEDS INDOLENCE DO WE MEET WITH THE PERFECTED TYPE. IT IS IN THE LAND OF ADVERSITY, AND OUT OF MUCH PAIN AND TRAVAIL THAT FINALLY EMERGES

5

THE HIGHEST MANIFESTATION.

NOT IN VAIN THESE WASTES OF SAND. AND THIS TIME NOT BECAUSE THEY ~~[illegible]~~ DEVELOP CHARACTER IN DESERT LIFE, BUT SIMPLY BECAUSE THEY ARE BEAUTIFUL IN THEMSELVES AND GOOD TO LOOK UPON WHETHER THEY BE LIFE OR DEATH. IN SUBLIMITY — THE SUPERLATIVE DEGREE OF BEAUTY — WHAT LAND CAN EQUAL THE DESERT WITH ITS WIDE PLAINS, ITS GRIM MOUNTAINS, AND ITS EXPANDING CANOPY OF SKY! YOU SHALL NEVER SEE ELSEWHERE AS HERE THE DOME, THE PINNACLE, THE MINARET FRETTED WITH GOLDEN FIRE AT SUNRISE AND SUNSET; YOU SHALL NEVER SEE ELSEWHERE AS HERE THE SUNSET VALLEYS SWIMMING IN A PINK AND LILAC HAZE, THE GREAT MESAS AND PLATEAUS FADING INTO BLUE DISTANCE, THE GORGES AND CANYONS BANKED FULL OF PURPLE SHADOW. NEVER AGAIN SHALL YOU SEE SUCH LIGHT AND

6

AIR AND COLOR; NEVER SUCH OPALINE MIRAGE, SUCH ROSY DAWN, SUCH FIERY TWILIGHT. AND WHEREVER YOU GO, BY LAND OR BY SEA, YOU SHALL NOT FORGET THAT WHICH YOU SAW NOT BUT RATHER FELT — THE DESOLATION AND THE SILENCE OF THE DESERT.

JOHN C. VAN DYKE, <u>THE DESERT</u>,
SCRIBNER, NEW YORK, 1901

PABLO NERUDA, <u>LET THE RAIL SPLITTER AWAKE</u>
(EXCERPT FROM THE POEM)

WEST OF THE COLORADO RIVER IS A PLACE I LOVE.
I TURN TOWARDS IT, WITH EVERYTHING THAT LIVES IN ME,
WITH ALL THAT I WAS, AND AM, AND BELIEVE.
THERE ARE TALL RED ROCKS, MADE STRUCTURES
BY THE SAVAGE AIR WITH ITS THOUSAND HANDS,
AND THE SCARLET SKY AROSE FROM THE ABYSS
INTO THEM TO BECOME COPPER, FIRE AND STRENGTH.
AMERICA, STRETCHED LIKE A BUFFALO HIDE,
AERIAL, CLEAR NIGHT OF GALLOP,
THERE, TOWARDS THE STARRED SUMMITS
I DRINK YOUR CUP OF GREEN DEW

PABLO NERUDA

SKYSTONE

TURRELL
LYON

12 E 6
100
40
OIL
STEREOFLEX
ACCESSOIRES

Gloriamur in Spe gloriæ filiorum Dei.
ad Rom. 5.

EMBLEMA XII.

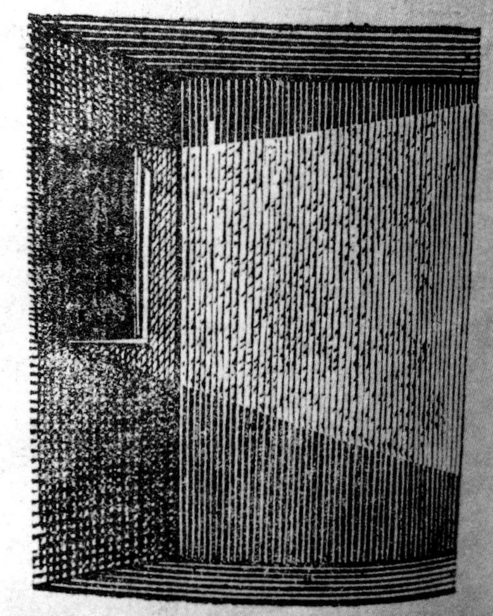

——— *Spes inſperata puſillos*
Excitat, & medio facit exſultare ſereno.

——— Euge, torporem excute,
Spatiare cælo, quoque Spes alacrem vocat.

Puſilla

Puſilla mens aſſurge. non patitur ſuos
Animoſa Spes dolere. ſit paruum licet
Cor, gaudio par eſſe non humili poteſt,
Vbi nocte Spes affulſit, & fecit diem
Etiam in tenebris. ———

Quibus Spes vitæ melioris affulſerit, poſſe eos etiam in tenebris & mortis vmbrâ ſedentes, feſtiuè exſultare.

INtus in obſcuræ tenebroſa cubilia noctis
Per tenues rimâ diſſimulante fores,
Si qua ſuperueniet quæ non ſperabitur aura,
Aura ſuæ lucis prædita deliciis,
Et vacuum pulchro diſtinguet inane ſereno,
Auricomâ pingens atria cæca face;
Ecce aderunt, hilareſque choros lætantia ducent
Certatim iunctis agmina pulueribus,
Gaudiaq; ad numeros veluti concordia nectent,
Gaudia feſtiuas ducta per illecebras.
Vſq; adeò noua lux animis gaudentibus apta eſt:
Lux adeò feſtæ præuia lætitiæ eſt.
Credo equidē, ex atomis ſi concurſantibus ingens
Naturæ tandem machina prodierit,
Cælorumque orbes, tellurisque ardua moles
Conſtiterit paruis edita corporibus,
Credo quòd affuſæ fuerint tunc omnia luci
Peruia; luxque ſuo quòd ſimul officio
Functa ſit, & leuibus faciens commercia pu
Iuſſerit hos pulchro denique ſtare mod
Quid tamen hæc Epicureo procuſa cer
Quid facit ad mores fabula Socrati

I 3

OUTLASTS VARNISH 2 TO 1
TOUGH ENOUGH TO SKATE ON®
2600

A classic lenticular cloud. WARREN WATSON

out over the center of the river. Then without warning the turbulence died suddenly, and I found myself climbing in that unearthly smoothness that can be found in only one place on earth – where the geostrophic wind curves upward in the leading edge of a mountain wave. I sat holding my breath, hardly able to believe what I was feeling as the rate-of-climb indicator slowly mounted to a reading of five hundred feet per minute and held there steadily while I maintained my course, now spanning the Columbia, now soaring across the brown hump of Burch Mountain.

After some impromptu acrobatics while I donned helmet and oxygen mask in the crowded quarters of the Laister-Kauffmann's cockpit, I found myself at fifteen thousand

Paola: Roden Crater, this big "ready-made" in the Arizona desert, whose edges you're shaping and in whose entrails you're going to create rooms to work with the light of the stars, the moon and the sun—I know it took a long time for you to find, but was there any special reason for choosing this area? James: Well, there were several. The first was that I wanted to find a place with a setting in geological time, time not of man's construction. And in this setting I wanted to make spaces and engage celestial events, so that what was made in light was something that was created by activity in the celestial vault. I was looking for areas that had little vegetation so that you felt the action of geology, or erosion, of time, time greater than the time our lives are involved in. Then I wanted something that was actually bowl shaped, something that really held you up so that you really felt yourself to be in the sky. And then I wanted to have an atmosphere where the clouds were not there all the time, because I wanted to bring these light events inside, so when something happened outside, it did something on the interior. With that I went to look for the space where I could do this, and I flew all over the western states. Each place I saw generated a new idea, a different idea, and so for a while I suppose these ideas were zooming out of control. But it was a wonderful period. *Does the light in this area have a special quality?* Yes, it has a brilliance, also there is an almost electric quality in the air at night. The crater is on the edge of the Painted Desert so the topography is beautiful as well. That has to do with the setting I wanted. I wanted a sort of geologically exposed earth so you felt the time of the earth. It's not timelessness. It feels a little bit like that in relationship to our lives, but it would be no different than our life as compared to a fly that lives one or two days. *When did you start flying?* Well, it was after I was out of the university. My father was an aeronautics engineer and early on he ran a technical school that actually built airplanes. But like many relationships of father and son, I was never interested in it while he was alive. It was not until after he died that I began to take an interest in flying. Before that I started building boats and sailing, which is why I like soaring. It combines flying and sailing.

Riding the elements like that feels alien to me. These fears are only learned, like an anxiety. It's different from real fear. *What is real fear?* Real fear is when you know the situation you are in very possibly will kill you. I think we have an understanding when we meet a lion or an animal of that nature. The species knows about it. It is not an instinct to fear flying. It is only by culture that we pass along the fear. These things are really not there. But I started being interested in flying in terms of the instruments, as I had been in sailing, that is, in actually making the craft. I do like to honor the things that help me make the flight possible. But I don't believe in planned obsolescence and I really enjoy things that do the work they do well. I do indeed like to revitalize these things because they are so quickly cast off in this culture. I come from Los Angeles, where in five years one easily considers knocking a building down and putting another up, whereas in Italy you can go through a village and if a building is less than fifty years old it's an exception. *Your mother was a Quaker and your uncle had an avocado farm, part of a Quaker community. Can you see some trace of this honoring of instruments, as you say, in the communal way of life you experienced as a child?* Well, I don't know. When I got a bike, it was one my father and brother would have purchased used and had fixed up so that it was in perfect condition and nicely painted. I came to like that because, obviously, I like these old things. I like that they've been used and they have a work-hard exterior, that is,

there are places worn from the work! Another thing to remember is that this ability to restore planes and to sell them is what got me here too, is what I earned a living at. I started restoring planes not because I enjoy antiques so much—it would be more comparable to people who perform old music on old instruments. It's a different realm in which you have the envelope and the nature of what existed then. I'm not interested in these things if they don't actually work or perform; I'm not interested for instance in the airplanes that are in museums, or in looking at old instruments at the musical instrument museum. They just sit there, and people can't experience the flight or the music. I like to give back life to these instruments and then put them back into the world. These things enlarge our territory or sense of territory, whether psychic or physical. But the possession of them can circumscribe our world and in a way make it smaller. This often happens with objects. To some degree that can even happen with art. The work can quickly

go from the studio to museum in such a way that it's almost embalmed; it becomes part of its death. But my interest is in perception, and that is a very difficult thing to exert ownership over. *And now you are going off for a month on a different sort of flight, gliding.*

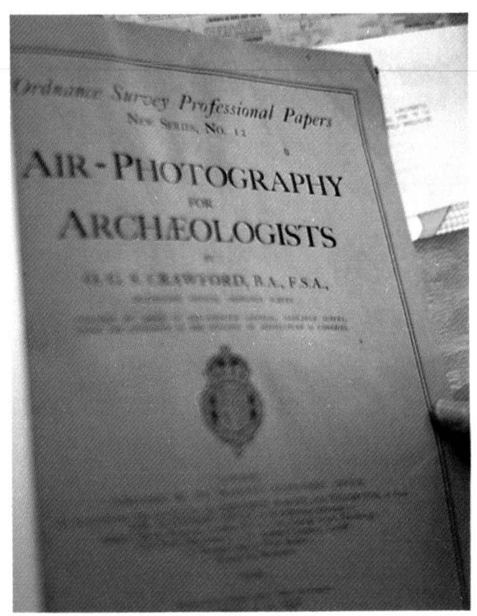

Well, now that I don't have to earn a living at it, I can do the flying that really has no financial return. It's the same with the crater. I could have an easier life in art if I didn't do these things, but they are the things I want to do. They have a lot to do with my measure of whether I'm doing it or not, doing it as an artist: accomplishing things that are not so much a measure of what other people think but what I think art is about. *What is gliding like?* Gliders look just like a plane only they have no motors. And with the sort of flight I want to make, that takes you up above 40,000 feet, you have to wear a space suit. The idea is to get near the jet stream and then go downwind. This is what normal jets do to fly fast across America. In the jet stream the air is moving from west to east at between 100 to 150 miles an hour. It sort of marks the line between the stratosphere and the tropopause. It affects an area of about 100 miles in width for a depth of maybe 20,000 feet and actually all the air around it, sort of like a rope pulled through a swimming pool. The water that is near the rope will be pulled along as well. *How can you see it?* Usually you can see indications of it, sometimes by reading the clouds around where it is supposed to be for signs of turbulence. The first indication can be the violent nature of the venticular cloud itself. The front

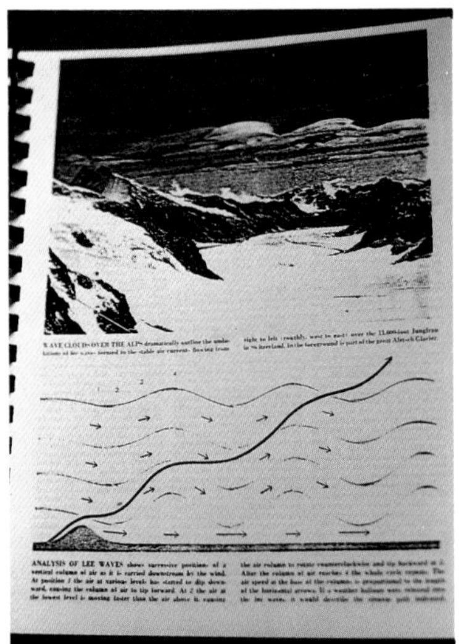

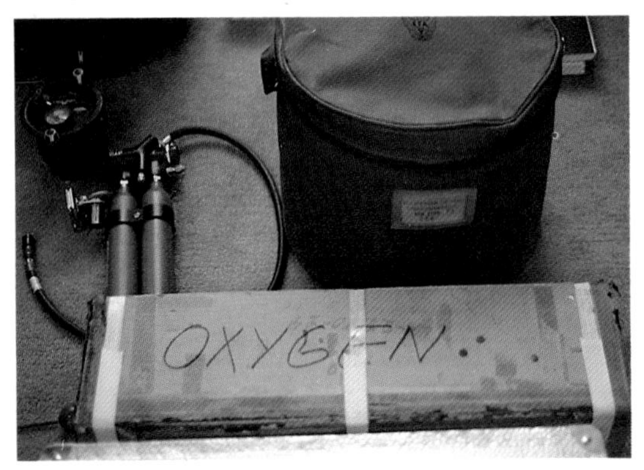

edge, the upstream part of it, can have pennants or little tufts. So the normally smooth venticular cloud is no longer smooth—it has rough edges. That's an indication of turbulence, but generally just indicating higher speed, and the jet stream *may be* above that—not necessarily. Occasionally, at high altitudes, when the jet stream descends, becomes a little bit lower, it can precipitate out clouds that are sort of cirrus bands. They look a lot like the large contrail of a jet. That's a very good indication of the jet stream, but you can't count on that happening very often. It's almost coincidental to be able to catch the jet stream. So first there is this idea of getting that wave and going downstream from wave to wave. You go up high, then descend downstream, hit another wave, go up high, descend, etc. You must have waves to get the altitude necessary to get near the jet stream. Then what I am really interested in is actually soaring near and in the lift created by the jet stream itself, since there are twists in it. I am going to try to do this right now, this month. You can do a long distance flight near the jet stream. In the fast-moving air that is near it. It doesn't have the problem of the shear and the turbulence. That is a good way to begin. *How long can the flight be at one time?* I have 24 hours of oxygen. It is hard to stay up for that long. Gliding at night is something you want to get together. If you fall out of a wave and don't have lift when you are coming down you need to pick out a place to land. Even though there may be a lot of light at the airports, the wingspan on the glider is such that if there is an airport that has raised runway lights because of the snow, and it is not wide enough, it could damage the wings. So of course I have to be very careful about the ones that I choose to land at. Some of the smaller airports downwind of these wave-places are not large enough to warrant a runway because where the waves and storm conditions are best aren't necessarily where they have the most population. In fact almost the opposite is true. The Great American Desert is tremendous for soaring, and there is very little population there. *And your work with light...* I remember when I was young reading *Wind, Sand and Stars* by Saint Exupery. He talked about spaces within the sky. As soon as you look up you realize the sky is not empty; it has this volume, is a sort of arena. As humans walking on the earth we are bottom-dwellers, no different than the fish that dwell on the bottom of the ocean whose eyes grow to one side of their head as they lie flat on the ground. Our perception is tunnelled by living on the surface, and as soon as you take off into the sky it's an amazing revelation of space. These spaces within the sky, what happens in the space in going from day to night, also what happens to the colors in the sky, are a source to me. *So you are actually trying to explore this other space, the sky?* The sky is not empty; its space is divided by a structure of clouds, and it has different structures within it, rising air, falling air, standing waves and thermals, that often are not really marked by clouds. *What about the perception of these spaces within spaces?* The interesting thing in terms of perception is that seeing is

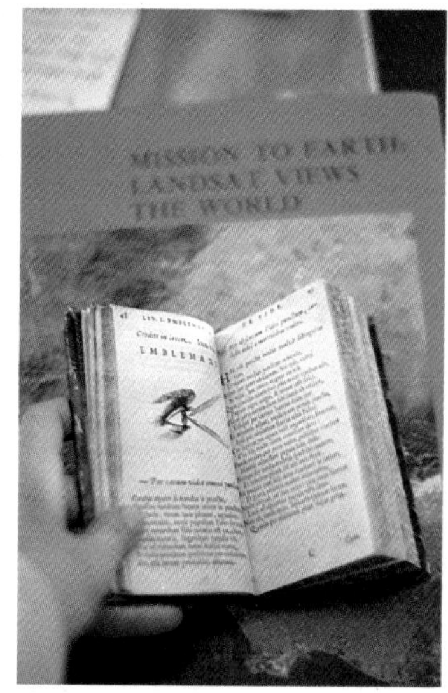

beyond the eye; it's not too much different from looking at what happens with dreams. Your eyes are closed, and you see quite well in a dream. In fact, in a lucid dream the color has an intensity that you see better than what you would see with your eyes open. I am interested in the superimposition of the imaginative space on the conscious awake space. There are times when seeing comes close to this. One of the things that happens is that, if the price of admission is paid, you enter that state. It's not so different from the act, the willful act, of reading a book that then puts you in the space generated by the author. You can look at art and not enter it; it's your choice. You don't need to start reading a book. But there is a willfulness in deciding to gain access or take entry. Sometimes you are so absorbed in that state that the people coming in and out of the room mean nothing. You are more in the space of the book than you are in the space where you sit. The place where you sit is now dissolved into nothing and this is a good example of superimposition, where imagining space is in fact taking complete precedence over the conscious awake space you are in. *Is there always this interacting of the outside with the inside through a shift in awareness?* "Totes interes, totes fores!" Everything inside, everything outside. *At your studio in Los Angeles you closed all the windows and blocked everything out for one year, then started slowly opening up. What was the nature of this project?* This closing off was basically to burn out light. There is so much light coming in here now; it's like trying to make music when there is a lot of sound and noise around. You have to take it down; then you can actually learn to bring out other sounds as well. It is very difficult for music to do that too. You don't find a lot of music out in a windstorm. With the complete closing off you see the seeing; it's possible to work with that. For example, when you close your eyes at night you obviously see color. In one of the pieces I made for the Museum of Contemporary Art, L.A., what you saw after sitting there for fifteen minutes was very much what you see when you close your eyes at night. You get that kind of color that buzzes and then disappears. In the piece you began to get the same image whether your eyes were open or not. Having worked with light, I then wanted to work in a natural surrounding and use the light that was there. And one of the nice things about the crater is that there is light there all the time. We know about working with clay or stone, making wax and making bronze; there's a quality of loving the material and working with material. For me the material is light. I become a lightsmith. Light is the material and the medium is perception. It was through light that I chose to work with perception because for me it was the most direct. If you are looking at paintings and you turn the lights off, you don't see them. You are working with light anyway; you are just working with it indirectly. Some of the paintings I like, for instance, by Rothko, Monet, especially late Monet, even Seurat, are about the act of vision, where in the act of looking at it the painting changes, as you move on it. Although Monet, as an Impressionist, was doing something interpretive, in the later work, particularly the water lilies and things of that sort, the paintings themselves were active to the seeing of them. This is true of Seurat's pointillist dots too, particularly as you move forward and back on them. Rothko was involved with light emanating from the painting as opposed to being reflected by the painting. This is also true

of Newman. Their work is about light but they used paint. I would rather work directly with light and not try to make the paintings something they can't quite be. It's a remarkable thing...like making a bird talk—but that's not like it's speaking. I am interested in going directly for it, which is an American approach. I don't want to hear the story, I want to experience the story; I don't want to watch the football game, I would rather play it. For this reason I am interested in work that engages you, the viewer, so it is not so much about my seeing but it's about your seeing, and I set up the situation in which you can then see yourself seeing. It's about perception; it's not about documenting an event. The event is your perceiving it. For me painting is a European sport. When a culture begins you always rob from the previous culture. The Romans robbed from the Greeks, but the Greeks had robbed from the Egyptians. New forms always began with reference to the old; many of the early movies were photographed plays. My work works plastically in three dimensions, it engages three-dimensional space, works with it and plays with it much like a painter's vision in three dimensions. It is not really sculpture; it does not use form and matter to display space and thereby affect it. It engages space with more of a painter's eye, but make no mistake—it is not about painting! Going to the moon...*deus ex machina!* You have got to take the entire gross national product of a large nation—America—put it into this damn thing and send it up to the moon. We went there in 1969 and haven't been back there in the last ten years. As a performance piece it ranks with the pyramids. It accomplished nothing more than the act. That has some beauty also; I liked that. But we had to go to the moon before we were able to make an airplane that could be pedalled across the English Channel by human power. Now that to me is elegance. There is a kind of craft of "doing" in the arts, but you have to rise above the craft. It's not what you want to notice. When people sit down and play the piano, you don't think: god, what a machine, what an incredible machine the piano is. And it is a machine. But you don't think that; you just hear the music. *So you are more interested in the power of a space than in what is spoken in it, with what a cathedral is rather than why it was built?* We need religion to make the cathedral and we need war to make the rockets to go to the moon. There will be a time when we can just get things straight and make something straight away. *Driving to the crater yesterday over that river of*

magma that seemed as if it had just erupted, through that valley of fossilized ocean waves... hearing the wind... it felt very much like being in a cathedral. Is that one of the reasons why you chose this setting? Where to begin is very important because the forces you see are what is empowering you. I wanted a space that felt like it was in the sky, and you do feel that there. I wanted a place to engage the sky, and I don't think we need to fly to be in the sky. In the same way, perceptually, we don't need to go to the moon to be in space. The earth is as much in space as the moon, but we don't think that way. It has to do with changing context. For instance, you go to a museum and you confront a piece of modern art and it's not so much a question of liking it or not, but of wondering why it is being put in front of you as art. But there could be a situation where you were on the beach and this object washed up on the shore and you discovered it there, and it's incredible. You want to take it home and put it in your living room. *What spaces are you going to create inside the crater?* There are going to be twelve spaces altogether. There are ten that are empowered by light, then one is the bowl, which is the actual shaping of the sky. Another room is the music for the other spaces; in there you can understand the sheet music, what's going to happen in all the other spaces. In this room is a bath of obsidian. Underneath the bath is a metal parabolic shape—the same shape as a satellite dish—to collect the electromagnetic radiation that passes through the hole in the roof and the top of the bath. So if you look through the opening you will see an area studded with stars, and if you put your ears below the water you can hear the stars in that area. As the earth turns, this room is sweeping the sky, so you see and hear different stars. The rooms are like your camera. With your camera you take a picture; you can change the lens so that you have a wide angle or you can have a very narrow angle or a normal lens. Then you change the aperture so that many things are in focus or just a few things are in focus. Then you can change the speed of the shutter, so if there is something moving you can stop it. Film can be black and white, or color. You can choose to see tungsten light as white, or sunlight as white, or fluorescent light as white, or you can see infrared, or you can see infrared in false colors. You can put things that are cold in blue and things that are hot in red. Then once you take the picture you can even cut out parts to blow up. Even in printing you can bring up shadow or make higher contrast. In courts of law people use a photograph as proof of reality when every step of the way we chose how we wanted to see reality—it's a complete sabotage of reality. I am making something where you come up against reality and how you form it. You're walking and suddenly the sky is curved, but who curved the sky? Is it the

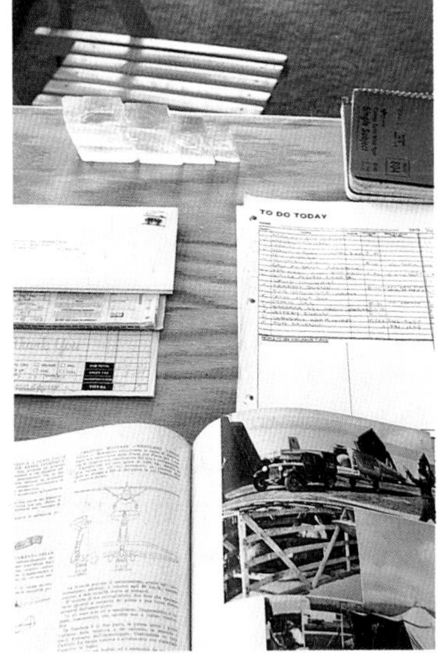

volcano that curves the sky? But in the end it's just a volcano. You're curving the sky! And, if you lie down, the sky is more curved than if you stand up. You can take a camera and turn it upside down—it does nothing because a camera is the instrument that determines how we see reality. It is just a fucking thing; all it does is tell us how we want to do it, but we are no longer conscious of the choice. This is what I call a prejudiced perception. We have learned to see a certain way and have then forgotten the learning. In fact, you decide to see things in, for example, a European way. You have a language that expresses certain things very well; other things it may not express as well. In ancient times great importance was placed on watching the cycles of the sun and the moon...to some degree these things are about knowledge, about knowing. But people honored these things because they understood these things allowed life to continue. The knowing was important and they honored the knowing. We are left with the knowing, which has become so prevalent, and I feel that not honoring this knowledge makes two things happen: we have increasingly better technological objects, but then the organization of society is on a downward curve. People like to look at things as progress, but I think progress is always something that is mixing and remixing and is a dangerous idea. So technology in no way helps society. All it's doing is helping to illuminate the problem. Better communication, better television—all this is making us see our problems better. It is not solving them in any way because it has nothing to do with the solution. Science is never going to solve any of these problems. In fact, it makes many of them. Science has no morality, and I think art has interest in this sort of honoring, and that is why it is interesting to me. People involved in art and literature, though they seem to lead an amoral life, have greater interest in examining this portion of human experience.

Enzo Cucchi

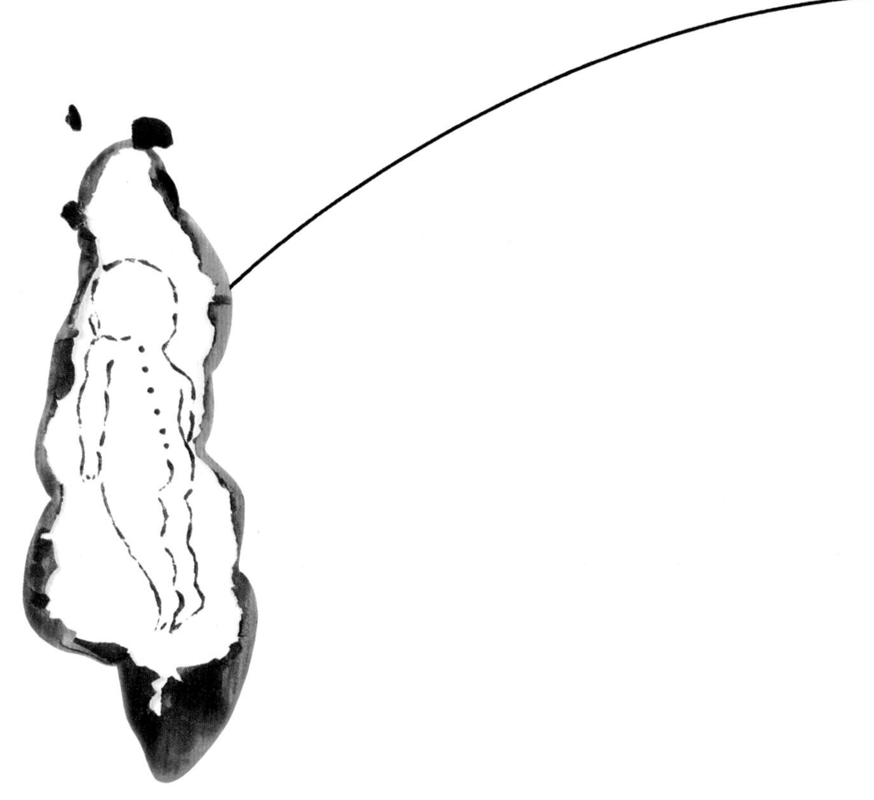

Position is important; it is the place where one meets to talk about something, observe it. But if one observes it from a distance, draws it, sings about it, one thinks one means the same things because one is talking about the same thing. An apple, a pear...their mystery lies in their weight, in their form; that is their meaning.

ENZO CUCCHI

Paola: The space around the artist can be his house, objects; it is that space in which obsessions, pleasures, things before transformation lie. Being a bit of a nomad, your space can also be internal. What is your relationship with everyday life? Enzo: That's not easy. It's like the sphinx—what the hell was it? All that was known was that it was anamorphic. A head. Then they began to excavate, and in the end they uncovered the whole lion. They saw that it was tranquil, that it had a peaceful face, gazing off toward the Nile valley, that it was in a natural state. We now realize, well, at least I say this, that the lion could be the artist. At the time they were removing the sand, who knows, maybe they were thinking, "In what fauna does this animal live?" Whereas he lived in peaceful surroundings and co-existed in a natural way with everything else, even though everything else continued to think that a lion is clearly not an animal of the desert. My everyday life is like this; it's very simple. The artist *is* everyday life. He is true everydayness, the one truly responsible for everyday life. And the others—they live in it, they can't handle it, they don't like it, they think it's bourgeois, provincial, or, I don't know, the usual thing. The artist instead *is* everydayness. So at times people create the problem of not tolerating the artist because he represents the everydayness of life. It's like the farmers who cannot stand their own fruit, the smooth-skinned fruit. They hate their pears and apples and refuse to eat them, but still they care for them, and this in reality means that they don't hate them. They care for them and they love them, because if they didn't exist then the fruit wouldn't exist. Just the same, they not only don't eat them, they also have a very hard relationship with them. Artists are like these fruit farmers, when speaking about everydayness. It's not that they don't safeguard everydayness, quite the opposite! They are very tied to it, but on first impact, it can at times seem like this. They don't eat it, they don't want to taste it, they don't want to know anything about it. That's the way it is. A painting, the work, you do it to do it. What is the ideal space to do it in? What is its place? Where is the image placed? A painting is done for that, not for other reasons. It's better to give up, if it's possible to do so. In fact, one must always think about giving up. *So there is always the relationship with time as well.* It's *only* related to time, and space is related to time and, thus, the most incredible everydayness is truly the concept of time. That's the way it is. It is an obsessive mirror; it is a vice, a prejudice, a bitter prejudice. Then there are the street lamps, the streets at night, those too are

prejudices. That has to do with time as well, not in order to stay out of time, because we are never out of time, but in order to stay out of everydayness, out of practical everydayness. Such are the street lamps illuminated at night. They absolutely do not have to be places...places of damnation. They are places to detach just that everydayness of the artist, of the artist as an idea in respect to people, because in that moment there is no longer any practical everydayness. For the artist everydayness comes like this: it is not easily tolerated because there are practical things involved; there are the everyday things, real matters, tied to social problems...that the rest of the world thinks the artist doesn't have. They think artists do

nothing, whereas the incredible reality is that they are the only ones who work today. They are the ones who really work, and it is the rest of the world that doesn't work, that doesn't do anything in a sense, that no longer has any rapport with things. It becomes dramatic. Writers and journalists don't understand anything anymore. *The simplicity of everyday relationships for you is having habits, having places where you work continually?* I *am* the habit, because there is only that for me, there is nothing else. First, it is a condition. You *are* a habit, that is why you find yourself doing certain things, thinking certain things, because you are a repository of these habits, not because you have decided it. I would like to do something else, obviously. But for me this is the only condition that I know. Other things I can look at; I would like to appreciate them, but I can't. Instead, what I do I don't like doing, but I do it. *The houses you have are always very essential; external and internal work spaces that continually change. Does that have a meaning?* It simply means that I can't stand the idea of boredom, something habitual, a real obsession, that is, in the sense of true reality, of everydayness. It is clear that if you built yourself a place that changes with society, that changes with customs, with tastes, it is never a place. No, it's not that it isn't; it is a place for people but not a place for the world. Thus it is not that I build houses or set up studios outside. I work here and there. This is because I am not able to do anything in any other way. There is no other way! Another way exists if you have the fortune to be truly not tied to things but attached to society. Society, at its best, is a decorative vice for saying things. This is not necessarily a judgment against society, but I am not able to relish it. What can I do about it? *In a certain sense you have always been a bit of a nomad. You have very deep roots, and then there is this space between the roots and this nomadism, the space where the transformation takes place, where the seeds brood, the obsessions, the dreams. How do these things co-exist?* It is very difficult to explain the transformation you are talking about. Everything that is not easy is usually also quite serious, but everything becomes more evident from how other things arrive, certain other human functions, certain rapports between beings. You never know where an artist comes from, from which meteor he was catapulted, what his starting point was. Thus, the only serious thing to think about is to think that he has this strange "Hellenism," this quality of Greekness, which moves a bit...this quality of the South, this Mediterranean quality of lightness and movement...and to think that it's through the work of an artist that he arrives. Because a painter always passes through the body of other painters. To look obsessively for this "Hellenism!" There isn't time. The time is absolutely missing. In fact, how can you finish a painting? You never finish it. You never know when it's finished. That is the problem, and that is why one continues to do them. But it is clear—the incredible goal is that of knowing how to live. I think of giving up, being able to find a moment of true renunciation, and this is why one is an artist, but this will never happen and there will continue to be artists. *The materials you use in your works, these pieces of wood, these things you find...* I use them as I would a problem of light. I do not use them to touch them. There is a whole modern art like this, I know. They have touched the materials in order to transcend them, to intervene on the materials. I have never intervened on the materials; for me the idea of intervening on the materials is unbearable. I am interested in the presence, like a creature which is there where the light falls. I am only interested in it in that sense, not to intervene. I only wish I had this vice of society; it's beautiful, radical. Then you have artists who like painting, who love to paint, and this is the reason why they love touching things. I do not like to touch them at all; it disgusts me, but it is clear I respect them. I don't know if one could call it this, but I feel them as if they were a presence. *These materials are like props. But do they have their own life?* Their own life because they are themselves. Painting, this painting is not absolutely necessary, not necessary, never has been. Why? Why did Giotto do what he did and not choose a Byzantine or other style? Why didn't he make another choice, and for what reason? It is not enough! He had an incredible freedom to choose among thousands of different styles. Instead he chose a strange path which now gives some relief to old men who are dying. *The opposite of aesthetics?* Yes, of course. Because if he had to deal with aesthetics he would have chosen, as I said, the Gothic style or the Byzantine style. At the time there was a whole range of certain half-styles to choose from. Instead he chose a certain thing—he tried to bring in some history, some history inside himself. This is strange. *Is it always difficult to define these things?* Yes, because it is not even necessary to define them. Because that day when they are defined the artist will realize it, and on that day it will be incredible and everything will truly end. That is how it will be. The artists will be immensely happy, they really will be, because I think that the transformation of materials relates to…the external—it does not relate to the painter. But it is also clear that in the transformation there is no longer the problem with the thing, with materials. The day this happens the artist will be liberated, exorcised. Yes, some priests should come into painting, but no priests can be seen, nothing can be seen today. Look at the critics who are always searching for young artists: this purity, in intellectual houses, in places…in cinemas…in various bivouacs…places where they think one might be, but they never go there to look, to see, that there might be something else in other places, people in a different guise—not in a different guise but in an ancient one…immediately easily recognizable. As you see, there is this deep vice, so when this great thing happens, this exorcism, perhaps it will be the artist again who will realize that the others are on the outside…then all the chatter they make will be useless. Where does it lead to? Nothing is understood. That is, no one understands anything; they always understand something else. And we are continually giving them material…to do things, what can I say? To make things, draw conclusions, go forward in this strange, radical thing, step by step. It is a form of social illness, in every sense. They don't understand one thing well: the work they take to be a rebellious action…I don't know, revolutionary…then they adapt it, making it into something else. Then it becomes a social slogan. It lacks mystery; it lacks form, specifically because it has been born from a completely different stomach. It would be as if I went around like a madman—if I were to go on a trip with a suitcase, and instead of a suitcase I took a large leaf from a tree and shaped it into a cone to put my things into, and I travelled with that, no customs agent in the world would let me pass. It's not the right container. It's unrecognizable. *What is your relationship with the home?* I am only able to half fill it. A house is only half-filled, never full. Thus, as you can see, one must also give up there, that is, give up everything, give up the idea of a house as the idea that it could represent who knows what, could be complete…you fill it by half. But at the same time you can have a global vision, understand?…of everything, because in the other half you can travel: this "Hellenism" we were talking about. There is air. There is time. There is space. Thus we must say it, that houses have to be only half-filled, nothing more. Architects are a symbol of a mentality…they are "far out." They actually think you have

to start to build from the roof down, so convinced are they that it is full, that they can walk on air. And they are truly convinced that this limited part of the house that the artists have as an idea is wrong. For an artist the house is always only half-filled, whereas the architect treads this empty area which for an artist remains empty forever. The difference is crazy. *You said that you've worked for a long time in these abandoned buildings here.* Yes, it was right after the earthquake; they've become earthquake studios. They were the ideal studios because the people were fleeing—everyone was running away—and what better place to set up a studio than where people have run from, understand? The artist's studio must be exactly that, a place from which people have fled, where they've really run away, where they suffered a trauma...a strong trauma, of fear. What remains is the presence, and artists always work better near the presence, be it in the mountains or by the sea. Why do you think the artists of the past worked outdoors? They also worked near real presences. Light: Cezanne. What is light if not an intermingling of presences? A place where people have fled from, where there has been a true exodus—it must at least be that. But the studios are not the studios of those of the Eastern bloc who flee to the West hoping to find a real studio. It doesn't exist. Now when we all flee to the East, what will they do? Will they follow us? All return once again to the East? I want to do a book with only one drawing, which is like a theater, and the whole book is a spoken monologue. It's a monologue with myself, by myself, like a madman, which will be titled "A Letter of Western Dissent." Yes! "A Letter of Western Dissent." Only one drawing, with a man seated at a table...two men seated with their spinal cords exposed and a falcon flying above to peck one of the spinal cords. This is the heretical position of the artist. *You said earlier that one truly works only travelling, in these suspended spaces.* Of course. What can one do staying still? Nothing, except rest. *This fascination of the seaport...it's one of the most incredible things.* There is everything in a port. There is the concept of escape, that of return, and it is the opposite of artists, who can never return; that is why it's so beautiful, right? *Did you have these dreams as a boy?* I never dream incredible things. *No? You never had these visions? What is the vision you can remember from when you were a young boy?* Nothing! I don't remember anything of when I was a young boy. I remember absolutely nothing. I don't remember anything at all. For society it is they who remember who are the artists. For society it is they who dream and relate their dreams who are the artists; it is incredible. If we say that we don't remember anything, it is a problem for society. We must recount our dreams, but we don't remember. How can we describe our dreams if we don't remember them? That's the way it is.

Vito Acconci

WILD PALMS

So it wasn't just memory. Memory was just half of it, it wasn't enough. But it must be somewhere, he thought. There's the waste. Not just me. At least I think I don't mean just me. Hope I don't mean just me. Let it be anyone, thinking of, remembering, the body, the broad thighs and the hands that liked bitching and making things. It seemed so little, so little to want, to ask. With all the old graveward-creeping, the old wrinkled, withered, defeated clinging, not even to the defeat but just to an old habit; accepting the defeat even to be allowed to cling to the habit—the wheezing lungs, the troublesome guts incapable of pleasure. But after all memory could live in the old wheezing entrails; and now it did stand to his hand, incontrovertible and plain, serene, the palm clashing and murmuring dry and wild and faint and in the night, but he could face it, thinking, Not could. Will. I want to. So it is the old meat after all, no matter how old. Because if memory exists outside of the flesh it won't be memory because it won't know what it remembers so when she became not, then half of memory became not and if I become not then all of remembering will cease to be.

—Yes, he thought, between grief and nothing I will take grief.

William Faulkner

THIS IS JUST TO SAY

I have eaten
the plums
that were in

the icebox
and which
you were probably
saving
for breakfast

Forgive me
they were delicious
so sweet
and so cold

William Carlos Williams

THE THREE PENNY OPERA

The world is poor, and man's a shit
And that is all there is to it.

Bertolt Brecht

LAST YEAR AT MARIENBAD

X's Voice: The park of this hotel was a kind of garden *à la français* without any trees or flowers, without any foliage...Gravel, stone, marble and straight lines marked out rigid spaces, surfaces without mystery. It seemed, at first glance, impossible to get lost here...at first glance...down straight paths, between the statues with frozen gestures and the granite slabs, where you were now already getting lost, forever, in the calm night, alone with me.

Afterwards the music rises and prevails.

Alain Robbe-Grillet/Alain Resnais

VITO ACCONCI

Vito Acconci was born in New York City. He loved horses since he was very little. His favorite hero was Roy Rogers. In school he was very smart. He got the highest average in the third and fourth grades. His birthday is January 24. He was born in 1940. He now lives at 2504 Bathgate Avenue, Bronx 58, New York.

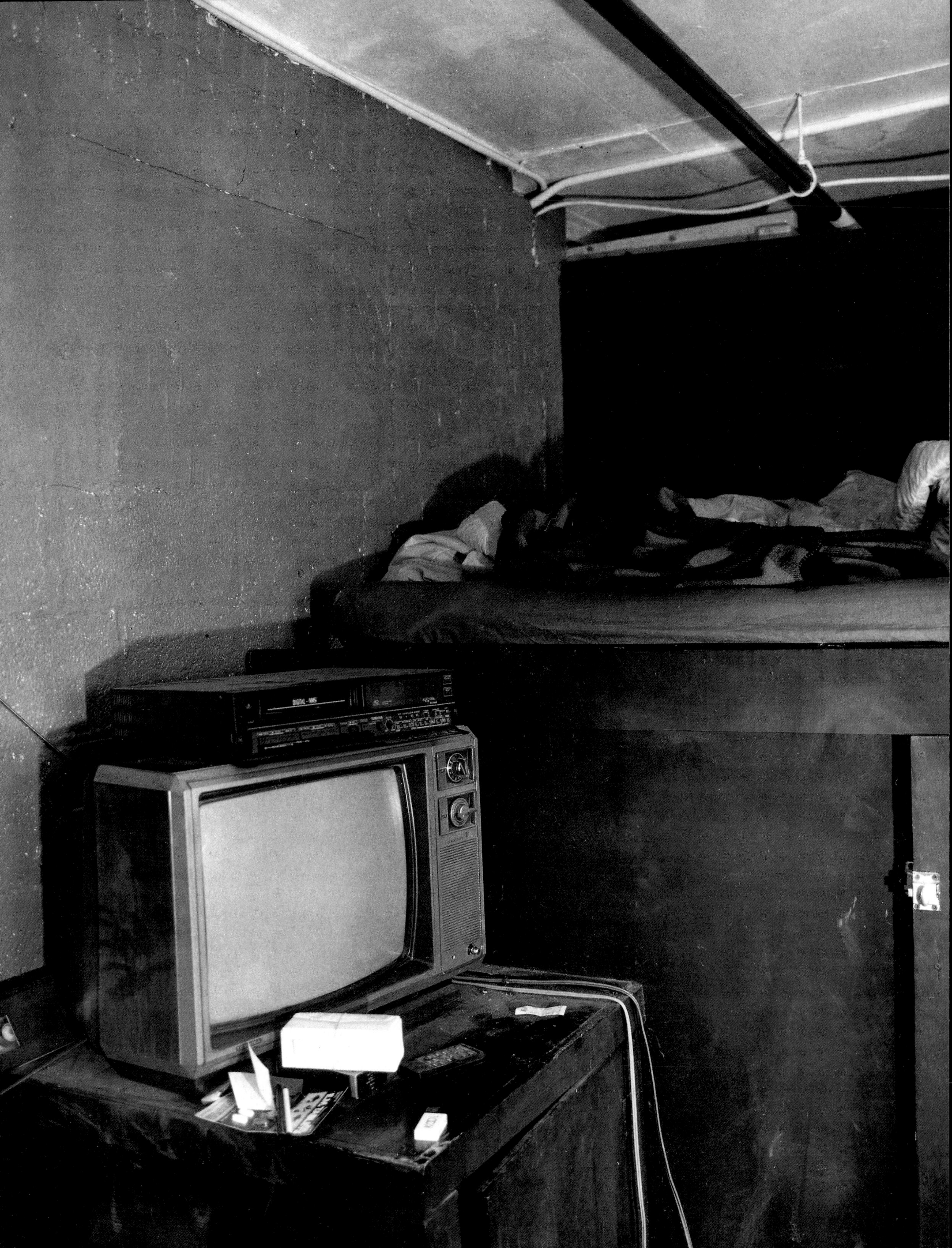

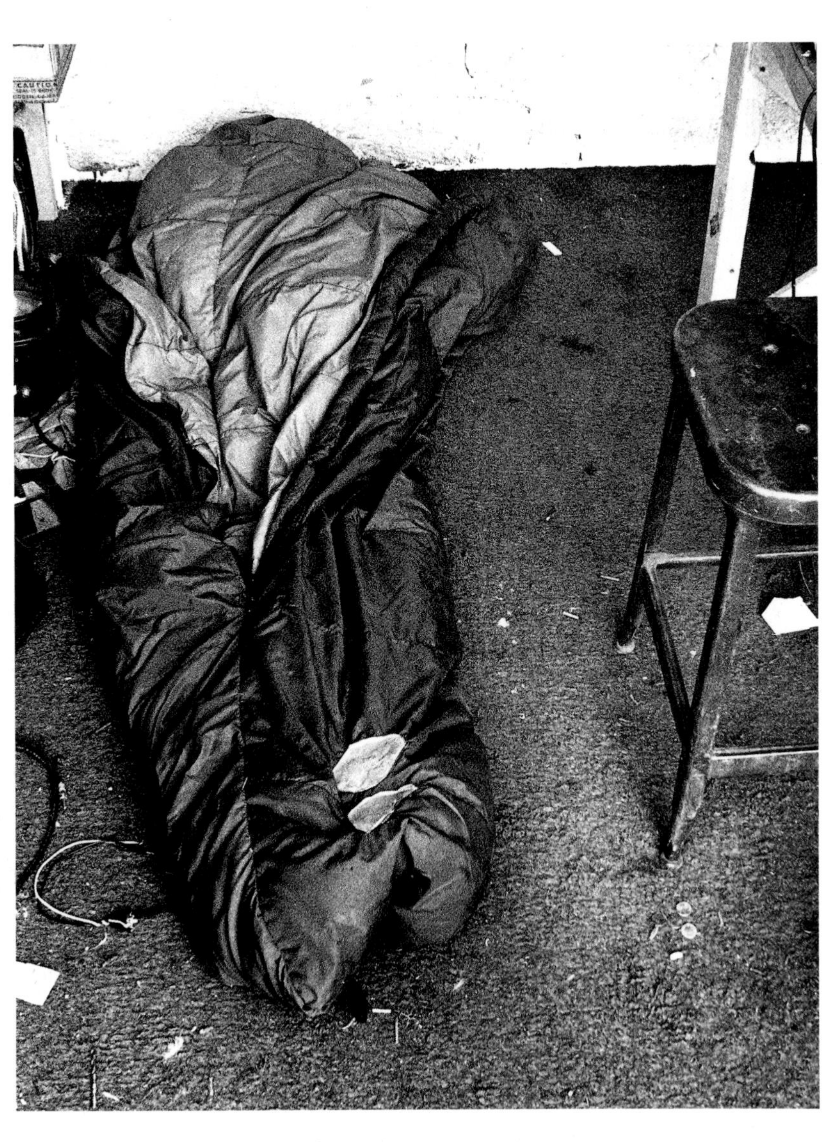

Kodak

BELGIUM
ITALY
172
206
WORKMAN PUBLISHING
s.point
Schleich
Art. Nr. 7.1002
Sportwagen
Sports car
Voiture de sport

PIER 17

ELMO
ST-800
SOUND
PROJECTOR
MAGNETIC

1
"Stories and Lore of the West"
1.
Horses
The Palomino must be gold to be genuine.
The Arabian could be white or *black, and they know the desert better than any other horse.
The Cayuse is the cowboys mostly used
*They are usually white.
western horse
Stirrups
open stirrup
Bits
barbit
spade bit
curb bit
Spurs
army sp
spanish or cow spur
Brands
running iron
hair brand
types of brand marks
6
This is a lariat with the "hondo" through which the rope slides.
Here is a ten gallon hat.
Here is the pack which goes over the saddle.
Here is a pack saddle
A halter does not have a bit. It is used only to lead a horse or pack mule.
"Along the Grand Canyon Trail"
by Vito H. C. Acconci
Jim Reid
Susan Blake
Sid Co
It is the time of the Civil Wa
The year: 1863. The place:
Charleston, North Carolina. In
home of Confederate millionai
Jonathan Reid, and his son, J
Jim said, "Father, I thi
it is about time for me

legs" from
thorny brush

ten-gallon hat is the cowboy's crown.

the neckerchief, called "wipes" in the early days.

the fancy shirt is mixed with Indian and Mexican designs.

tooled leather belt and handworked silver buckle are mexican style.

gun belts cut wide are called buscaderos.

usually, holsters are custom-made for the guns.

gloves are used to prevent rope burns.

wide chaps, called "bat wings" +

spurs

...e heel
... in
ground.

the boots high heels helps the cowboy to rope a steer, or any other animal *

Correl says, "Here I'll lend you my gun." Jim says, "Why, Correl?" Correl says, "You'll need it to kill that horse." Jim looks at his old horse and then shoots him. In town he buys a beautiful Palomino stallion. He and Correl buy new clothes. He goes to the fort with Correl. He meets Correl's beautiful girl friend, Susan Blake.

PARTICIPATION/RELATION
(1) LIFE-WORLD
C: CUSTOM/CULTURE/SYMBOL
PARTICIPATION/RELATION
(1) LIFE-WORLD
A: GENERAL THEORY
AMERICA
ARTICIPATION/RELATION
(1) LIFE-WORLD
D: FAMILY/GROUP/INSTITUTION
PARTICIPATION/RELATION
(1) LIFE-WORLD
B: SELF/SPACE/INSTINCT
PARTICIPATION/RELATION
(1) LIFE-WORLD
E: PERSON-TO-PERSON
MAN IN THE TRAP
BODY

HISTORY (4): AMERICA
HISTORY (3): WORLD
HISTORY (5): NOTIONS OF DOCUMENTARY
IRREGULARITIES & EXTREMES
(1): STRESS / CATASTROPHE
SUPERSTRUCTURE (1): ECONOMICS
IRREGULARITES & EXTREMES
(3): CRIME & PUNISHMENT
A: DETECTIVE NOVELS &
GANGSTER MOVIES
IRREGULARITIES & EXTREMES
(2): DISEASE / INSANITY / SUI
IRREGULARIES & EXTREMES
(4): WAR
INTERNATIONAL
LESLIE FIEDLER
RACE
TO END WAR
CRITIQUE (2): COUNTER-CULTURE
& UTOPIA
CRITIQUE (3): REVOLUTION

BODY

BODY (2): ANIMAL/VEGETABLE

MIND

MIND (2): EXTENDED MIND

A: MYTH & RELIGION

TIME

TIME (2): FUTURE STUDIES

TIME (3): REVISIONS OF PAST

TIME (4): SCIENCE-FICTION (NOVELS/STORIES/MOVIES)

SPACE: LAND

MATTER (1): THINGS & PRODUCTS

MATTER (2): FOOD

PHYSICS

NUMBER (1): MATH & LOGIC

NUMBER (2): MUSIC

STRUCTURE (1): ARCHITECTURE

A: DATA/MODELS/GRAPHICS

B: ~~INDIVIDUALS & TYPES~~

A: MAGAZINES

B: HISTORY & THEORY

C: INDIVIDUALS & TYPES

FORM (4): PHOTOGRAPHY

COMMUNICATIONS & MEDIA: (1) THEORY

COMMUNICATIONS & MEDIA: (2) NEWSPAPERS & MAGAZINES

COMMUNICATIONS & MEDIA: (3) [illegible]

C: CITIES

D: VERNACULAR

E: SPECIALIZED

F: EXTRAS

STRUCTURE (2): FURNITURE/INTERIOR DESIGN

STRUCTURE (3): CLOTHES/FASHION

INSTRUMENT (1): MATERIALS & TECHNOLOGY

INSTRUMENT (2): ENGINEERING/INVENTION/DESIGN

INSTRUMENT (3): VEHICLES/TRANSPORTATION

INSTRUMENT (4): TOYS & GAMES

SIGNS (1): THEORY

SIGNS (2): PRACTICE—(LANGUAGE)

SIGNS (3): PRACTICE — (CODE)

FORM (1): ILLUSTRATION & GRAPHIC DESIGN

FORM (2): CRAFT & ORNAMENT

FORM (3): ART

THOUGHT & EXPRESSION (3): PHILOSOPHY

NARRATIVE (1): FICTION

(A): COLLECTIONS & MAGAZINES

NARRATIVE (2): MOVIES

HISTORY (1): ARCHEOLOGY/ANTHROPOLOGY

HISTORY (2): THEORY

HISTORY (3): WORLD

ORGANIZATION (1): LISTS & DATA

ORGANIZATION (2): WHOLE SYSTEMS

THOUGHT & EXPRESSION (1): POETRY.

(A): COLLECTIONS & MAGAZINES

(B): INDIVIDUALS

THOUGHT & EXPRESSION (2): JOKES/ ANECDOTES/ ESSAYS

ADDENDA: MEDIA—"DIRTY BOOKS," "DIRTY MOVIES," ETC

PARTICIPATION/RELATION (2): THEATER

IRREGULARITIES & EXTREMES (1): STRESS/ CATASTROPHE

IRREGULARITIES & EXTREMES (2): DISEASE/INSANITY/SUICIDE

IRREGULARITIES & EXTREMES (3): CRIME & PUNISHMENT

(A): DETECTIVE NOVELS & GANGSTER MOVIES

IRREGULARITIES & EXTREMES (4): WAR

(A): FILM & FICTION

SUPERSTRUCTURE (1): ECONOMICS

SUPERSTRUCTURE (2): CASTE/CLASS/ RACE

SUPERSTRUCTURE (3): POLITICS & GOVERNMENT

(A) FASCISM — FACT/FICTION/ MOVIES

(A): GENERAL THEORY

B: SELF/SPACE/INSTINCT

C: CUSTOM/CULTURE/SYMBOL

D: FAMILY/GROUP/INSTITUTION

E: PERSON-TO-PERSON

F: SEX & GENDER

CRITIQUE (1): THEORY

CRITIQUE (2): COUNTER-CULTURE & UTOPIA

CRITIQUE (3): REVOLUTION

~~[illegible]~~ (A): MEDIA & PROPAGANDA

LAVA
AIMEE RANKIN
AS FAR AS THE EYE CAN SEE
Idea
Image
KAWAMATA

Paola: Your work is about stretching the limits of everydayness. How does your actual daily life fit into it? Vito: I'm in the middle of a very large space; all the living parts are shoved into one corner. It's almost as if one of my car sculptures would be a perfect place for me to live. I've nothing like a couch. I've nothing. It almost seems as if I want discomfort. I don't want to sit in chairs; I sit on the floor or pace around. That obviously has something to do with my work. *You have plants here, I see, and a fish. How do you like taking care of things?* They come from some of my pieces. When I was a child, the only pet I ever had was a little goldfish in a very small bowl, and the fish just went from one side of the bowl to the other. The bowl was about seven inches and the fish was three, four inches. So the fish could do nothing but turn around, and the water got green, and the fish was orange and it looked very nice in green water. Since then I have had only this fish here from an old piece. The other fish were kept by people who seemed to like to keep fish more than I do. I don't know what to do; I can't throw the fish away, but I don't feel very comfortable keeping fish. *You said that this fish here, at some point, had another little fish companion but they didn't seem to get along.* Another fish was brought in—a friend thought that maybe the fish needed some kind of company. This was a big tank and the fish maybe had too much room. This fish was relatively big, seven inches long, a goldfish, large and slow, and we put in another little fish that was very different. The black fish was small, thin, had bulging eyes, and was very fast. I liked that fish because it looked a little like Peter Lorre in *The Maltese Falcon*...it looked like a kind of *film noir* fish. The goldfish was very much out in the open, but the black fish liked to be sneaky; it always tried to go to the bottom into the corners. The strange thing was that they seemed to be in totally different worlds. One was a goldfish, the other was a black fish; neither knew that the other was a fish. I mean how *do* you know? They lived in the same tank but in different rooms. At the Museum of Modern Art all sorts of little problems came up with the fish in my piece there, like whose job it was to take care of the fish: the preparators' department, the conservation department, the public relations department? Apparently, the public relations department takes care of fish—visitor services! Conservation takes care of plants. *In your recent work—the house of cars, the bad dream house at the Modern—there are all these spaces that really displace you from a familiar way of being in them, but at the same time they go back to an internal, house-like constriction.* They are usually places for more than just one person, so that they are not necessarily private. It's where you and other people are almost too close—almost unbearably close. Now something has to happen: you can't

stand to be this close, so either you get closer and you totally withdraw or else you have to break out again. You're so close you really can see the other person. You have to touch, smell, hear—it's like other senses come into being. It's what New York is like, because you can't see New York; you are always in the middle of the city. You experience it more than see it. You feel buildings around you but you can't really see them, which is very different from the way Chicago is built. In Chicago, it seems you always see vistas; it's like the city is built to be seen. It's in a way like what you said about children's drawings—that girls draw things face to face, boys from above. It's very difficult for me to have something built totally in another place; I have to be there so I can see it as it happens, so I can keep changing it at every step, and then it's like I can't leave it alone. When I start a piece it's almost as if I can see it from above because I begin a piece by drawing, or I might make a little model. But when you start to build it's very different—now you're in the middle of it, now you're face to face. You can only see one part at a time, so you can't see it as clearly as when you were above—everything seemed perfect then, everything was in order. It seems that once a piece starts, then I begin to think, "Now what I really wanted...." It's as if I want the model to be perfect, but I want to screw up the real thing. *I'm thinking of you as a child, living in a really small place, feeling you had to get out of it all the time, or play-acting in it and filling it up. Also your memories with your father were about taking walks together.* There was always the Sunday morning walk, always a walk, but then we would always come home; I would go out with my father and then come home to my mother. It was very strange. In childhood there are probably two ways of going out from a small space: one is to go out mentally and to make some kind of metaphor, some kind of fiction, as when, in the middle of this small house, you make a kind of theater, a make-believe, bigger world; the second way is to actually go out. Then the luxury of going out is that you know you are going to come back. You can't go out forever. *Where did you grow up and who lived with you at home?* We lived in an apartment building in the Bronx. There were four doors on the landing: diagonally across from ours, my grandmother, and then some strangers, an Italian-American family...they were always strangers. My mother would talk about family or strangers. Even if they were people she knew maybe better than she knew her sisters. They were still strangers because they weren't family. *That's sort of enclosed!* Yeah...and very much an Italian-American way, or at least the way I grew up. There is such a fear of leaving the house. My mother calls me everyday between 11 and 11:30 p.m.—usually between twelve minutes after eleven and twenty-five minutes after eleven—and she always asks, "Did you go out today?" Which is a rather strange question. My mother doesn't realize how strange the question is. It seems to imply that going out is, first of all, a real effort, almost as if you have to take a deep breath. Outside the home there are strangers; outside the house there is a wild uncontrollable world so you stay inside and obviously that's had an effect. You put the house upside down, you tear the wall off but at the same time, I wonder…I probably spend a lot of time alone and therefore inside the house. I wonder if a lot of that hasn't persisted. I wonder how much fear of the outside I still have. *What about make-believe? Either you go out and tear the house down, or you do this make-believe. Did you ever make a sort of theater as a child?* Every Sunday afternoon. My father, my mother, and my grandmother would be the audience. *Did you improvise or was there a plot?* It was continued week to week, like a soap opera, really a combination of a soap opera and a Sunday football game. I was the only child and had to do all the parts. Because I didn't have brothers and sisters, I depended on a fictional world in a lot of ways. *Tell me about Billy Schmidt? Does he still exist?* How do you know about Billy Schmidt? *It was mentioned in* Avalanche. Sometimes he comes back. The name is real—he was a person I went to elementary school with, but not a real friend, so I'm not sure why I focused on that name—I think in part because all the other kids at the school had Italian names and "Schmidt" sounded so good for a baseball player. But then he eventually started to play other things. He played football. He did a lot of things. *So who exactly was Billy Schmidt?* The real one or my one? *Your Billy Schmidt.* Well mine was and still is…he became a baseball player after high school; he didn't go to college. I don't remember where he went to high school; I don't think I made him go to the same high school I went to. In some way he had to be different; he had to be a real "other." Then he became a superhuman baseball player: he was an outfielder, he was a very strong home-run hitter, and then he gradually built this incredible career in which he would hit more and more home runs every year. He was the same age I was, so when I started he was seventeen years old and he got older the same way I got older. He played baseball for years; then he also played football, of course. He was a quarterback. He was always in the central position—always in the dominant position. Very often during the baseball season I would follow him almost every day—how many hits he'd have on a particular day. Baseball is like a kind of soap opera—you don't have to be good everyday because there is always the next day. *Would you think about him every night when you went to bed?* I would review my day and his. *And so even now sometimes at night when you go to bed he comes back?* Not so much anymore because by now he is retired; he's too old to play baseball. But he played for a long time. I guess I got bored at one point. Because he was such a super-human player, there was an assassination attempt on him. It's perfect because outfielders are alone. They are just three

people far, far off in the green. He was a perfect target, so someone tried to shoot him, but I can't exactly remember what happened. Then it got tremendously complicated; he started having this amazing personal life. After a while he started to see all these women, and they were all either actresses or popular singers. He would see every actress I was interested in. Then it was strangest when he was apparently seeing three very young girls at the Palladium. There was even a court case because he fucked all these fourteen-and eleven-year-olds at the Palladium. It got a little bit outside of baseball. Then also he became a movie director and he did a pornographic baseball movie but I never followed that through enough, so I don't know enough about the movie. But it starred some baseball players who had just retired and they were now porn actors. There were lots of things about bats and gloves and "driving the ball." After the porn baseball movie he made another movie, a Western, a very long movie that is still unfinished. It's about ten hours long; because it's about landscape it has to be very long. Jodie Foster was in it, and the movie was a connection of American pioneers and the invention of baseball. As the pioneers went across the country the covered wagon would stop and they would get out...and there would be a lot of land...and somebody would throw something...and they would start playing baseball. The Jodie Foster character was a kind of narrator. She was from one of the pioneer families and she was still pretty young. Jodie Foster is probably too old for this part now. The movie went on for a long time; she got older. Of course she was a girl child and so would always watch, because she wasn't allowed to play baseball, but, when the men were tired of playing the real games, she would occasionally start to play. Although she had this urge to play baseball with the men, she was trying to start her own baseball game. But she could never get it going. None of this was ever written down; I never followed it through carefully. *The idea of the center comes through in your work and your life—wasn't Billy Schmidt always at the center of the game?* When he played baseball he was the center-fielder, then he was the quarterback, then he was the movie director—it's the same thing. *Like when, in your performance, "Watch," you became the clock; you can feel that you were an only child. Did you start writing early on?* As a child I used to make these little magazines. They were sports magazines on the one hand and magazines that had something to do with Westerns and cowboys on the other hand. Like in any sports magazine, there would be stories about famous baseball

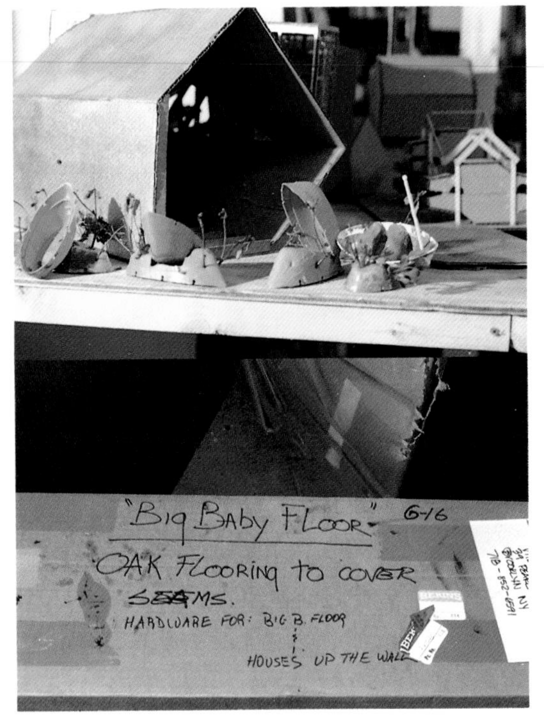

players—this was 1948—and there would be drawings of baseball players, and sometimes a little poem about a baseball player. And in the Western magazines (my mother still has one) there would be a story, always the same, always about two brothers, and they usually took place in the Civil War, and one brother fought for the North and one for the South. It was always from the viewpoint of one brother. I think they always ended at the same point: as soon as the hero met a woman all of a sudden the story ended—all of a sudden you turned the page and there was no book. It's like I was stuck. I could talk about the Civil War…I wasn't there; I could talk about cowboys…I wasn't there. But women—I didn't even know how to start making that up. That was a fiction that was totally beyond me. But the Westerns…part of the magazine was a story and then part was an attempt to write a kind of lore of the West, and there would be drawings of different kinds of guns, of a spur or a holster. There could be this fiction only if there was at least some kind of illusion of fact. I hate vague mystification, but I like the kind of mystery that comes from very clear precise things. You can turn precise things upside down and you'll find a mystery. But there must be the things we know first; it's really important for me that you have to start with something that everybody knows—you start with a window, you start with a house, a car, with something that isn't private. Then maybe you can do something to it and make a different thing. I think that was true when I was making the little Western magazines when I was eight years old. *That sounds like the way I'd imagine a screenplay would come together.* An interesting thing about screenplays comes up in *The Big Sleep* that Faulkner worked on. There's this scene with this rich person who is very sick; he's always in his hothouse in the middle of a lot of plants. I'm not sure if it's this way in the book, but in the movie it seems so Southern. All of a sudden it becomes a scene out of a Faulkner novel; then it changes and becomes something else. For like the first five minutes of the movie you are in this moving Faulkner world, but the screenplay was actually written by three different people; it's as if Faulkner wrote the first scene and then went away—it's very strange. *You like Faulkner, don't you?* Faulkner was my first big hero. What I liked is that he could never make a sentence end, as if a period were so drastic, so final, that you had to try as much as possible to avoid putting one in. So you put in a parenthesis, you put in a subordinate clause. You try to delay putting that period in because once it's there, it's over! Somehow, I feel that is still important to my work. I also think that Faulkner's method possibly has to do with the way I work because it's very difficult for me not to make changes. Significantly, my first two writing heroes were Faulkner and Flaubert. Flaubert had this kind of perfection, this something that only existed as a book, that was almost rarefied, that was between the covers. These two aspects keep coming back. *What about Ezra Pound?* Well, yes, Pound was tremendously important; his urge for perfection attracted me because at that point I didn't

Now he reads: "Then he jumps out of his skin."
Then he jumps down his throat.
He is, then out from under.
He saves his skin then.
He has a thick skin now and then , he says now.
and then he says it again: "I have, too."
And the rest is left to be read into.
He does it right.
He does it right off.
He does it in his own right; it's his skin.

I am here.

I am here as I go by.

I do it, go into the other.

I do without it, stop outside.

A knife (a knif-
er at it)
Cutting this out, that's you, and cutting loose
now as you cut through this, as cutting across, there you are,
cutting in, here you are, at bit
(a bit still on it,
a forkfull) a fork

(here) (   ) (   )
(   ) (there) (   )
(   ) (   ) (here and there—I say here)
(   ) (I do not say now) (   )
(I do not say it now) (   ) (   )
(   ) (then and there— I say there) (   )
(   ) (   ) (say there)
(   ) (I do not say then) (   )
(I do not say, then, this) (   )
(   ) (then I say) (   )
(   ) (   ) (here and there)
(   ) (first here) (   )

He was small page 1
Until after he was growing up page 2
For a while he was growing page 3
As well as much as an page 4
Inch at a time by page 5
The time he would look on page 6
Each occasion until as time page 7
Passed each had gone page 8
By as he went past them page 9

have it at all—I had to pare down. At the same time there was William Carlos Williams—a kind of Americanness, a kind of conventional everyday speed that I think was important for me, particularly because of my name. I knew I was American, but I had such an Italian name. *I like the Hannibal in your name: Vito Hannibal Acconci.* When I wasn't writing poetry anymore I dropped it because it seemed like "this is a poet's name." It was a time when artists were calling themselves Bob Rauschenberg, Bob Morris. Vito Hannibal Acconci seemed from another culture, another land. It was sort of important for me to try and find out what is American...I grew up as an Italian prince. My father was born in Italy; my mother was born in New York of Italian parents. My father never became an American citizen because that would have been un-Italian, but he never went back. *You were saying that your father was interested in puns. He made a lot of puns.* That's how I learned language, from my father. *That's what I thought. Probably wanting to cover the space of the page in your early poetry, that freedom, is also rooted to being outside the language and having a different language.* When you're outside a language you can see how language breaks apart and transforms itself because you don't make assumptions, so you see this word and all of a sudden it's two words. It's much easier to see that when you're on the outside. I've noticed that when people are foreign-born they seem to be much more aware of the language; a particular language seems much more mysterious, seems like magic, and you focus on particular words more, whereas if you are used to using them you go right through words. My father read only Italian books. He embedded me in the world of art, writing, music, but it was only Italian art, only Italian writing, only Italian music. At one point I remember telling my father that Wagner was better than Verdi; my father wouldn't speak to me for a week. *Where was he from in Italy?* L'Aquila. *That's in the center of Italy. You studied classics in high school?* Yeah, I did classics in high school and college. Homer seemed so primitive and raw. I was drawn to the primitive and raw. Virgil seemed literary to me, so by extension Latin seems like the literary language; Greek seemed like an attempt to get at root meanings, an attempt to get at the beginnings. I have a feeling what I saw as manner and decoration in Virgil would maybe be more interesting to me now; it's almost as if Virgil would be the post-modern version of ancient languages. I like Catullus. *You told me you went to college in Iowa.* Yeah, I went to graduate school in Iowa. I had this Woodrow Wilson fellowship I wanted to use. I found out about a creative writing program at the University of Iowa, so at the last minute I decided to go there. From my Bronx childhood and adolescence, I now landed in the middle, literally, of the United States. I mean, I didn't know what the midwest was. To me, at that time—Iowa, Utah, Idaho, Ohio—they were all the same; they were all those names that had a lot of I's, O's, a lot of vowels. *How was it?* It was flat, unpeopled. The people there walked slowly, talked slowly, and from what I could tell, thought slowly, or

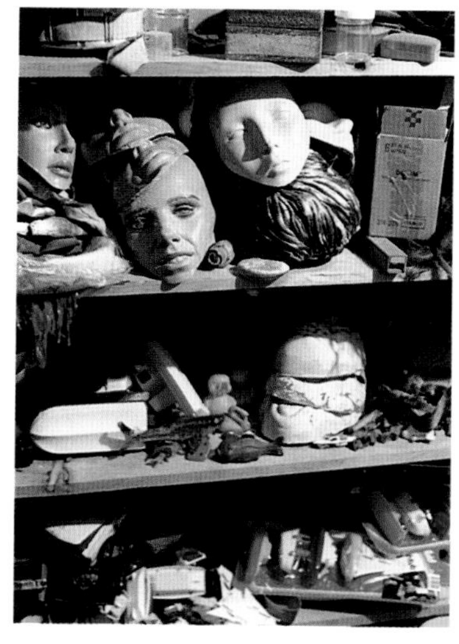

gave the appearance of being very, very silent, very uncommunicative. It seemed that they were always looking in front of themselves and all that was in front of them was grass. There were no people, there were no incidents. Every once in a while a car passed by, but mostly there was grass, and they watched it grow. The first year there I was considered a real outcast. At that time, in Iowa, the writing standard was *The New Yorker* and the *Esquire* short story. My heroes then were Robbe-Grillet and Beckett. They were enemies in Iowa. In other words, New York was the enemy. I remember a writing teacher who said to me, "I think Robbe-Grillet is toilet paper." And I remember that same person, referring to Beckett's *End Game,* once said while giving a class, "Do you realize that at this moment in New York City people are paying money to see two actors on the stage in garbage cans?" *And what was the first thing you published?* I published some short stories when I was in graduate school in some literary magazines and also through Olympia Press in Paris, which once had a reputation—they were the first people to publish Henry Miller, possibly the first to publish Genet (I don't quite remember). At one point they published a magazine, and they printed my first story. It was a story about a person who had no legs, whose wife had him put on the top of this giant ash urn, and she would always walk by and put out cigarettes between his two stumps. Because she really hated this amputee of a husband, she always wore dresses of fabric that made a lot of noise, so that he would always hear her wherever she walked. The story took place in one day—it was the wife's birthday—and the husband without legs had ordered a giant condor as a birthday present. The action in the story is mainly these moving men bringing in this gigantic ten-foot-high bird. At the end of the story, the guy without legs manages to open the condor's cage and throw himself into it. He's eaten by this giant bird as his wife is upstairs masturbating with a crucifix. So that's the kind of story I was writing when I was in college. *What were your early writings like?* When I came back to New York I started to have a lot of mixed feelings about narrative on the page. I started to write poetry. The first thing I published was a free version of the *Agamemnon* of Aeschylus. It was an Ezra Pound-like version of the classic; sounded very poetic. I was in a very mixed-up stage when I got back to New York. I had discovered things that had happened ten or fifteen years before, but they were very new to me. It was the first

time I had ever seen a Jasper Johns painting and it changed my life. I couldn't write the way I was writing; something had to change. There was such a notion of materiality on the canvas that I felt words...didn't mean anything; it was all imaginary. I was struck by the notion of something material. I was starting to get involved in things like idioms, conventional phrases, language that cancelled itself out. Language that you put on the page started to be about the page, more than it was about the kind of subject matter. *So the line in your translation of Aeschylus—"in summarized tonsils"—has a lot to do with what you were doing.* So you think I was trying to pare my tonsils down? Well, it's true, I was trying to be more precise—I wanted things to be harder, to be more material, less connected with flights of the imagination. I wanted things to be connected to the paper they were on, in the same way that the surroundings of a page act as a summary of what's on it. I guess I was trying to knock extras out. I was trying to get rid of anything unnecessary. I think I have always had that desire for my life, yet at the same time I live in an incredible mess. (laughs) *I notice that you have pockets of the things you like. All your records are packed together, and then you have a little closed room on the other side of this one and it's all books.* You should go look at the books; they are revealing. They're all categorized so that it starts with Body and then goes to Mind, but then—across from Mind, up there—there is Mind number two, Extended Mind, a more mystic thing. And then there is Myth and Religion, and then from Mind you go to Time. *"The Living Clocks?" What are the Living Clocks?* They were all books that at the end of the sixties seemed to be important—human time, biological time. Then you go to Time number two, which is Future Studies. I think I have sixty categories in all. There are things you have outside and things you have to put inside. Maybe this is the major piece! (laughs) Here is another section I like—Irregularities and Extremes: the first sub-category is Stress and Catastrophe; then comes Disease, Insanity and Suicide; the third is Crime and Punishment, and that's divided further into detective novels, etc. The fourth is War, in which you have war film, war fictions. After Irregularities, you have Superstructure, and then Economics and Politics. Then Critique and then Revolution. So I set up this whole world and then break it apart. I guess it's the same way I make work. I start with the body, the way I start at home, go to the mind, then to the extended mind. First the center, then

break it, then try to bring things together. You have a superstructure, then a critique, and then you have a revolution. *Do you live a lot during the night?* That varies. Sometimes when I'm writing I tend to want to write during the night, a more private time alone—dark and writing—it's that kind of cocoon-like activity and night is perfect for that, but other kinds of work I do all the time and any time. When I write I always handwrite, I can't write directly into the typewriter, and I write in a number of drafts. The first you can't read—it's gibberish, it's just scribble. It's almost like there's this illusion that if you keep the hand going and you make marks, you keep the mind going, and every once in a while there's a kind of intelligible word. So, it's as if you provide this kind of jungle, this forest, in which you can't see particular things but every once in a while, almost unconsciously, I make a word clearer. It's a clue that the next time I should focus on that word. And the next time maybe two or three words are clear, then four or five, and by the last draft all the words are clear. *It's like pacing around?* It's very much like that. It's like putting something in motion. Yeah, even though there's not even a thing in motion, it's more like it's the undercurrent that's boss. So that the word isn't clarified yet but you have something like this kind of river that goes underneath it and carries it along. And very often if I don't read it right away, I can't understand it. So it's not notes so much, it's more a kind of action of behavior. You get into a habit of how to think, so that the things you do while you're thinking start to seem almost as important as the actual thinking. So if you think while you pace, while you walk, it's almost as though, well, if you sit down you can't think. If you think while you smoke, then you think if you don't smoke then you can't think, because thinking is so hard to put your finger on. Thinking, where is it? Walking or a cigarette, at least that's something concrete, something that you know, that you can at least pinpoint and then you call that thought. When I work on a piece it takes me such a long time to get to what I want, it's like I have almost to feel the space that I'm going to work in, and since while I'm here that space isn't here, the space is elsewhere, it's almost as if going through that process of handwriting is an attempt to feel out something, almost like pretending the page is the space and making writing on the page equivalent maybe to walking around the space. *Making it physical.* Yeah, it's like making it. After a while, it almost seems like you make something physical; it doesn't even matter what

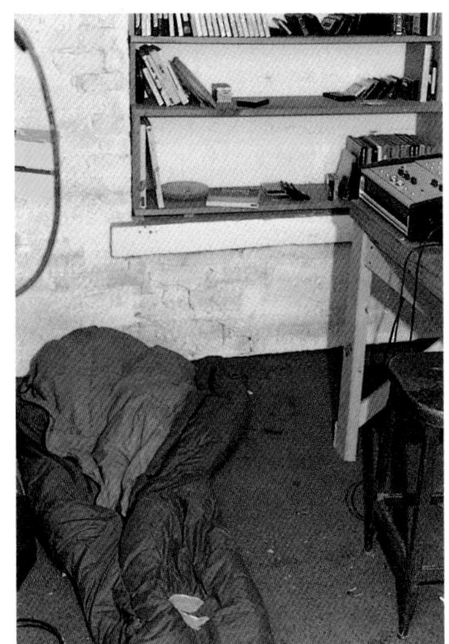

it is as long as something is physical. *Movies have meant a lot to you. Tell me about some of your favorites.* I wish I could pinpoint why movies seem so important. I know I get a lot of ideas from movies, but what I don't like about movies is the fact that they are always in front of you, you're always distant from them, you're in the dark almost pretending that you're not in a space. In other words, when you're in a movie theater you're almost supposed to forget that the theater exists, you forget that the seat exists, you drift off into this screen that comes off like a kind of dream world, and I hate that part about movies. The interesting thing about the dream world though is that it seems that when you think about the dream, you think about something very horizontal. It's something that stretches in front of you, a kind of expanse. It's almost like what the movie does is take this horizontal dream and turn it right side up, turn it so that it's vertically in front of you, and all of a sudden it becomes like a wall. When you think of dreams, you don't think of walls, you think of floors, landscape, meandering through, a never-ending landscape. Movies transfer that to a vertical screen, a wall. I'm not sure what that means, but periodically throughout the time I've worked, I've made films. But I've always felt that films were subordinate to the other kinds of things I was doing. The other things I was doing involved space that you walked through, the space you're in the middle of, but a movie is a space you're in front of. In spite of that, it seems like so much of the way I think comes from movies. There's an American movie made by an American director by the name of Tod Browning, in the thirties, called "Freaks," in which all the people in the movie except for one person are circus freaks and this one person is a normal woman, a trapeze artist. She marries this dwarf because she knows he has a lot of money. The rest of the freaks know that she's doing this in order to steal, so they start to exert this kind of revenge of the freaks. Everywhere this woman goes there's always a freak there. She climbs stairs, and there's a freak underneath the stairs looking at her from below; she walks by the side of the road and there's a freak up in the tree looking down on her; she's in her little cabin and she looks out the window, there's a freak in the window. Some of them can't walk, they're always crawling, they're always like part of the ground, they come up from the ground. And it seems like in a lot of work of mine there's always the notion of something underneath the ground, that you, the viewer, are on the ground floor. A floor is something that, in normal life, you assume is solid, you know where you stand, you have a sure, secure footing, but in some pieces of mine, when pieces work, it's like under that floor, something comes up. So the floor isn't as certain as you thought. You thought it was a whole and then suddenly it tears apart, suddenly a little freak comes up from below and it's an incredible thing for me. Just an incredible thing. *You also like the Godard movies a lot, don't you?* I love Godard movies. It's funny, with Godard it's almost like they're not movies, they're about movies, they're metamovies, analyses of movies, surveys of movies

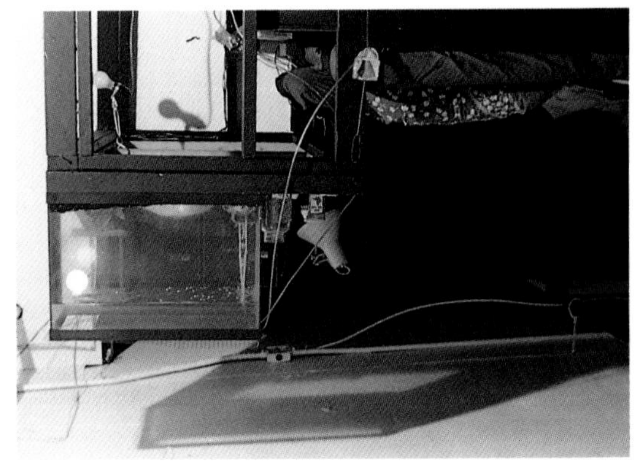

from another direction, almost like a movie as an essay, not as fiction, it's a movie that sort of talks about movies and presents movies. I like that part of Godard but I also like the fact that when he does the actual movie making he takes prototype scenes from other movies and makes them almost as blatant as possible, as cartoon-like as possible, it almost seems like making movies from the very beginning, making movies do the most obvious things in movies, do the most cartoon-like things. In a way *Contempt* is the one that got me. A movie is so much about landscape, and this movie has the great house, the Malaparte house, so that the movie becomes so much about a kind of landscape. There are these scenes filled with the shrubbery around the house, filled with green. And in the middle of the green is this kind of three-person relationship, two men and a woman, and it's in this kind of closure, the shrubbery is making a kind of entanglement in the same way that these people are entangled. But opposite this is this nothingness; from all this green it becomes this blank wait. The camera goes away from the land, and it just goes into this empty scene. You see absolutely nothing. It's as if Odysseus has come home and there's nothing there. The interesting thing about this "nothing" is that it doesn't seem hopeless. It seems like now that everything is pared away, now that there's emptiness, maybe this really is a new home, because the old home wasn't there anymore. Maybe this is like a different kind of beginning. Maybe in normal everyday life when you meet a person that you haven't met before, there's this kind of hope deep down that by means of being with this person, you are going to be transported to this other world. But the problem with relationships and with the person is that it turns out that when you're so close together everything else goes away. But as soon as you go away from that closure, that "both of us together," it doesn't hold up, because the world is filled the way you know it. Maybe that's the urge on the part of some people to do architecture, public space. It's almost like at one point you possibly felt that when you started to do art, you wanted to change the world, but you'd have no idea what that means. So, if you can't change the world, you could at least maybe change the shape of the world. But I don't believe the world can change just by making a poster or billboard or having a political poster. You're still in the world you ordinarily know. That earth has to change before the political poster makes sense. So I think the urge of people who do something like architecture is maybe the urge to shift, shift the ground, shift the land, shift the walls, and that's the start of a really political kind of thinking. *Tell me about the project in Washington State that you and Robert Mangurian went to see.* It's an artist-architect collaboration. The architect Robert Mangurian, the artist

Eric Orr and I form one design team, in competition with two other design teams, for an area in this college campus called the Glenn Turrell Friendship Mall. The notable thing about the school is that it is a land grant college, which means it began as an agricultural school, so there are some strange things on this campus. There is a cow with a window; they've cut the skin and they have a plastic-like cover so you can see inside the cow, and you can see the process of giving birth! The cow walks like any other cow; it's normal, it munches grass. They have this incredible building, a kind of science laboratory, where they have freeze-dried horses and freeze-dried sheep. But the best thing was some animal—I think it was a pig. I'm a city person; I don't know. *Was it pink?* Well, it didn't have skin anymore. It could be anything. It could be a chicken, it could be a child. If it was a pig, I was thinking of it as a kind of pig book because it was a combination of animal and text. The pig was cut in very thin slices almost like prosciutto, from head to tail. Each part of the pig was then put on a rectangle of plexiglass (so it's behind the plexiglass) and behind it is a text that describes that part of the pig. So all the parts are one behind the other, with the text behind its part. When you want to read it, you pull a slice of the pig to the right and now you can read the text and then you push it back in. It's incredible, the idea of a pig that can be read like a book. It's like this pig is an open book. *Will you show me the rest of the house?* This is the storage space. (Walking through a sequence of dark, tall box-like spaces with large boxes piled against each other, old works, and many small cardboard models of works.) Because I'm not good at drawing I always cut out cardboard and build little models for the works. Here are some. Here is the sound room. I was working a lot with sound in my performances in the seventies when I moved to this studio, so the most important thing was to have a sound room, but then I never made a piece with sound again. *So as soon as you made the sound room you stopped working with sound?* Obviously you make plans according to your past. That's the wrong way to make plans, but you don't know what the future is going to be. So... *This is a wonderful room.* It's a good room. Very often I come into this room because it's the most enclosed one. It's great; sometimes I can take a nap in this room because it's like total darkness. There is no outside. *You know, there is a slight echo. It's very weird.* *Is it really insulated?* Yes, but it doesn't work. It doesn't really work in that, although everything else is insulated, the floor is not. You hear constant noises from underneath. This was designed as the sound room, but it's the only room in the place where you hear people's voices for most of the time. The floor is cement. It must work as a sort of amplifier, it takes other people's sound in...that's what happens when you call something a sound room.

1. The [illegible] TV; in other words TV [illegible] privatizes. The [illegible] This [illegible] One other [illegible] Another other [illegible]

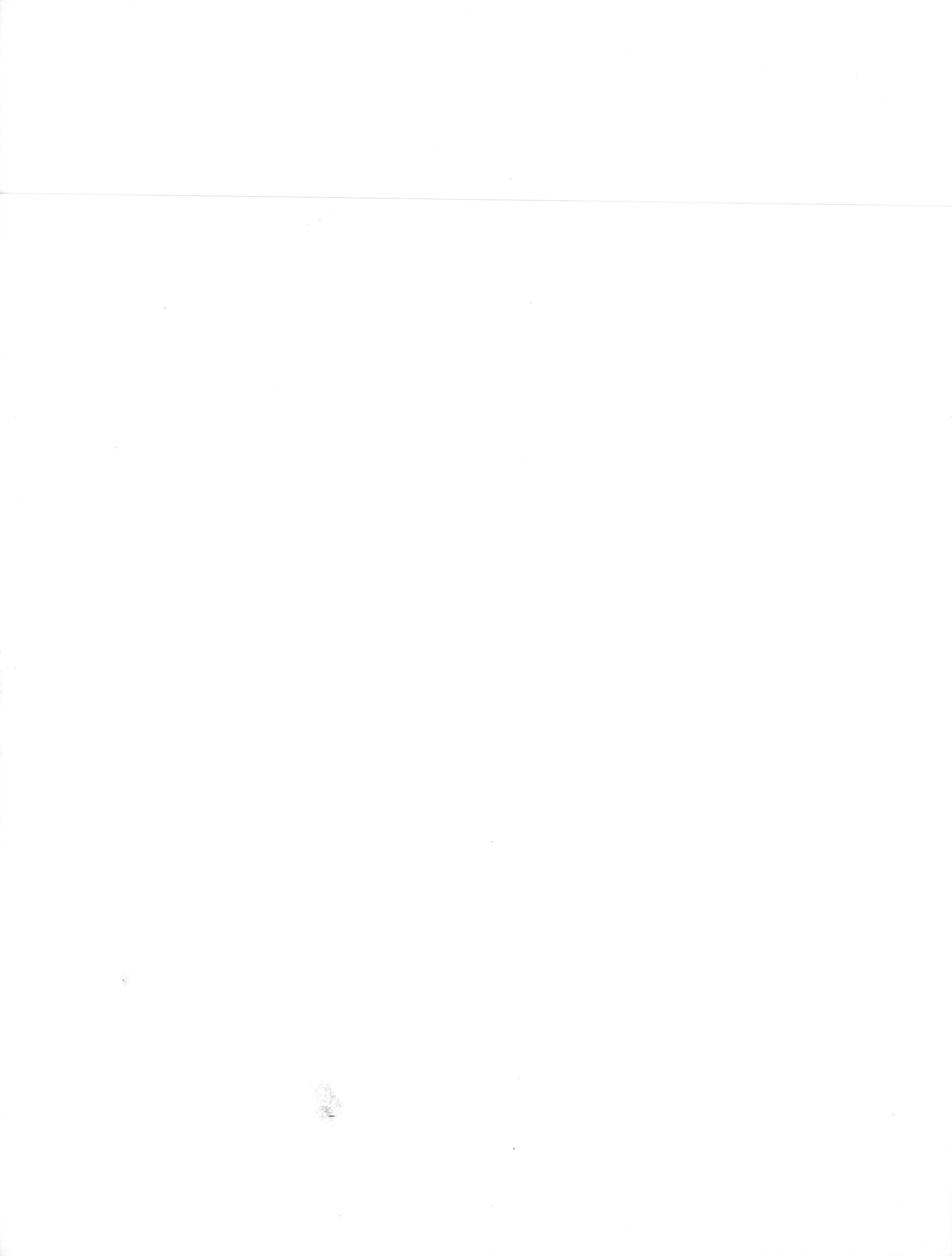

Cy Twombly

Archilochos

[this shred
of Alexandrian
paper, torn
left side, right side,
TOP and bottom,
& in the middle,
Reads]

you [

] if [

river [

] so [

I then, alone]

Aug. 29 1984

21 1985

Wilder

Shores

of Love

Quink
CONDOTTIERO
COZZO

TELEGRAMMA ◆ Amm.ne P.T. ◆ TELEGRAMMA
NNNN
CY TEOMBLY
VIADELHEREDITA 5
BASSANO/INTEVERINE
BASSANO IN TEVERINA

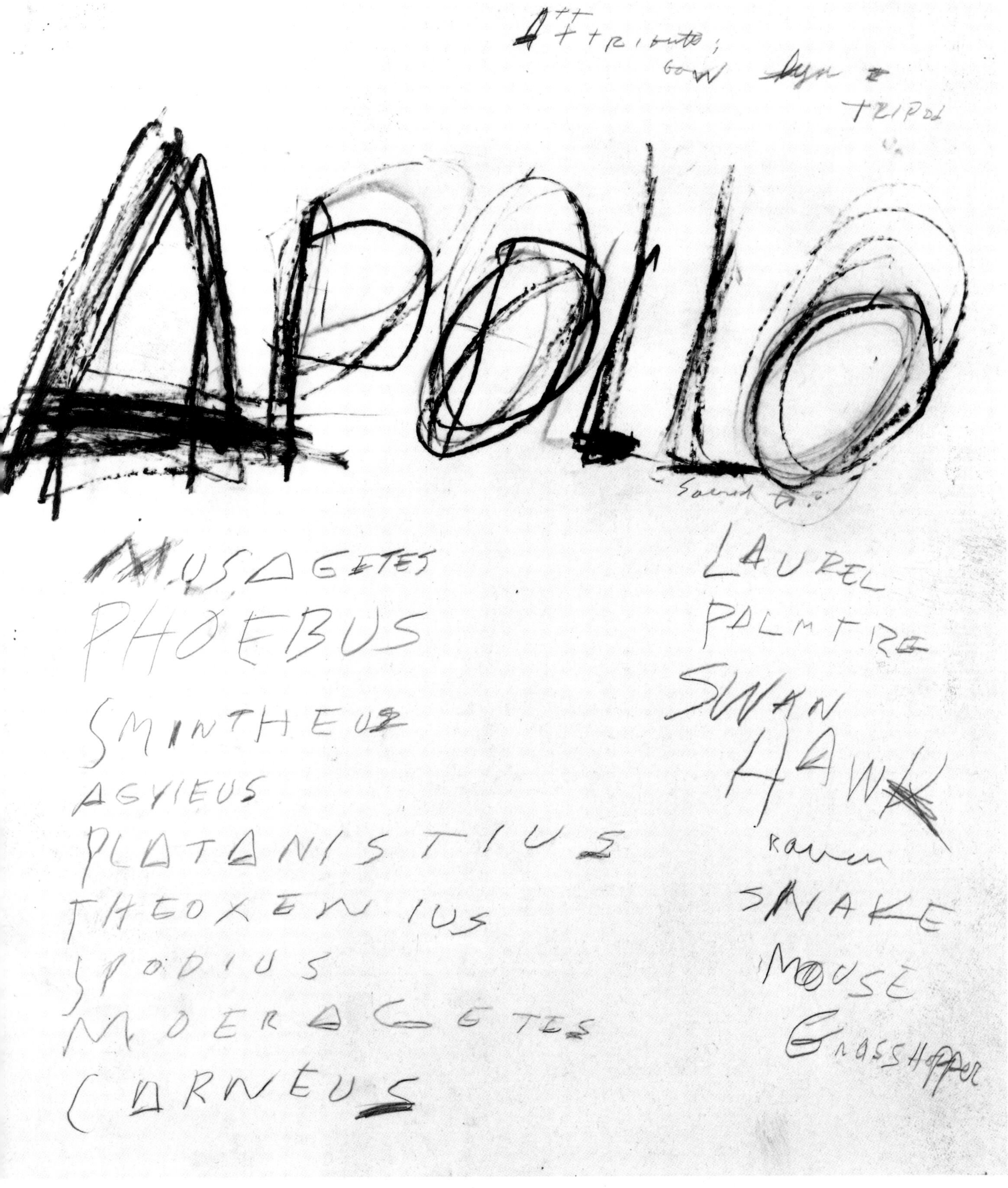

Attributes;
bow lyre
TRIPOD

APOLLO

Sacred to:

MUSAGETES
PHOEBUS
SMINTHEUS
AGYIEUS
PLATANISTIUS
THEOXENIUS
SPODIUS
MOERAGETES
CARNEUS

LAUREL
PALMTREE
SWAN
HAWK
raven
SNAKE
MOUSE
GRASSHOPPER

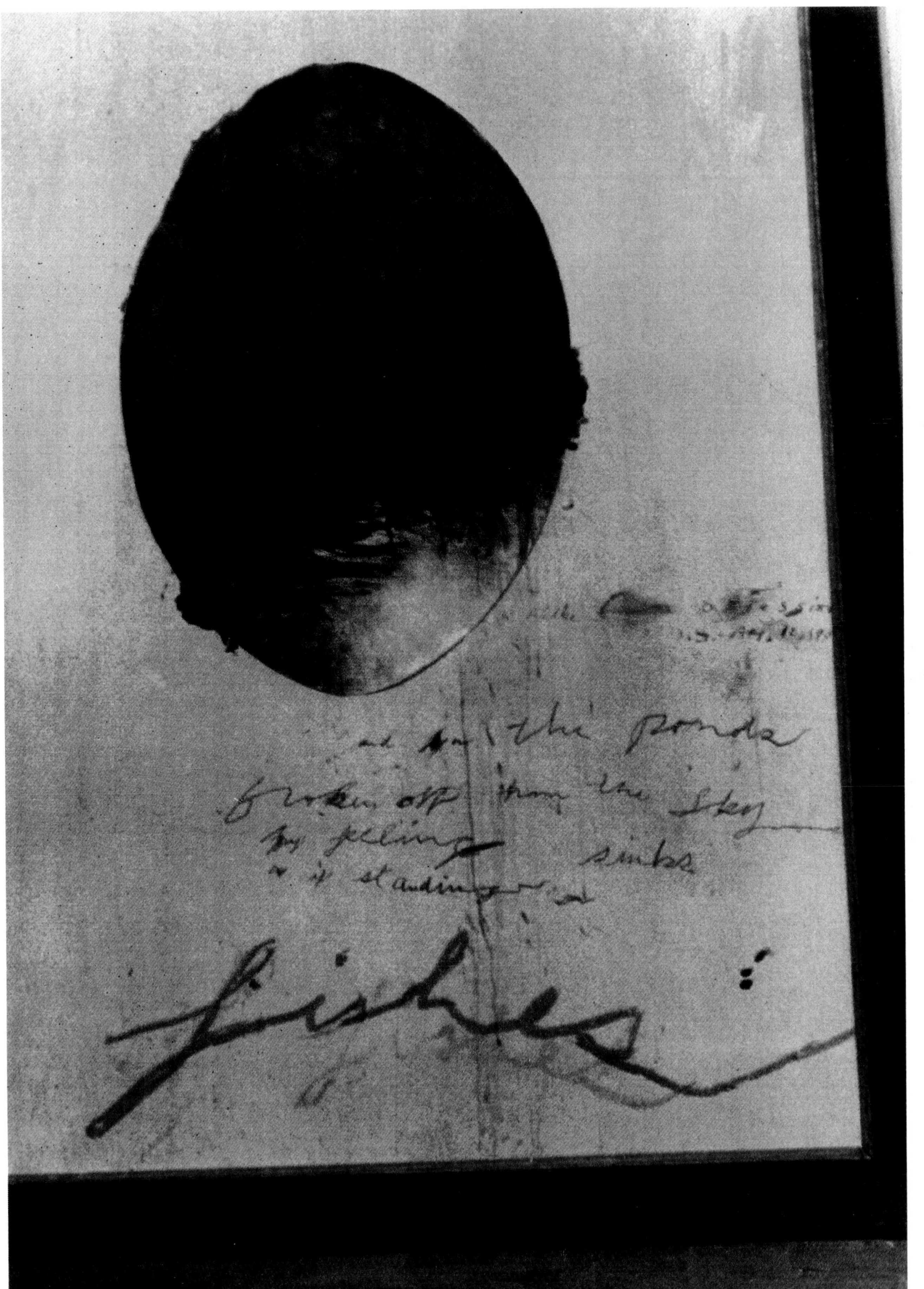
the ponds
broken off from the sky
sinks
fishes

ANABASIS
NOV. 20 83

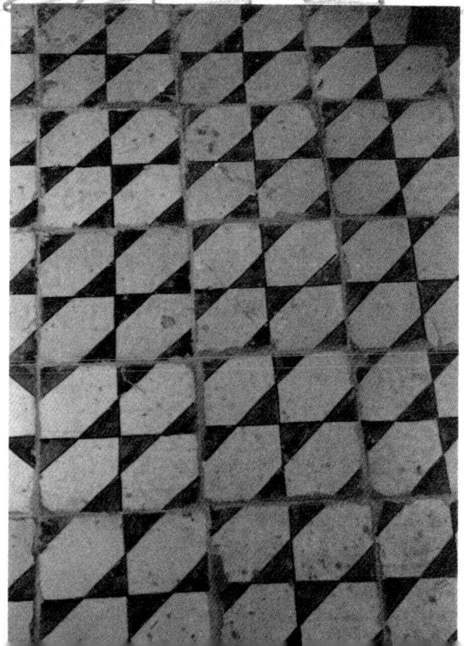

[illegible]
[illegible]
and [illegible]
[illegible] the
[illegible] and [illegible]
[illegible]
[illegible]
[illegible]
[illegible]
[illegible]
[illegible]
[illegible]

Gilbert & George

WE LIKE VERY MUCH TO BE HAPPY.

WE LIKE VERY MUCH TO BE DRUNK.

WE LIKE VERY MUCH TO BE UNHAPPY.

WE LIKE VERY MUCH TO BE SOBER.

WE DON'T LIKE VERY MUCH TO BE HAPPY,

OR NOT DRUNK, OR UNHAPPY OR NOT SOBER.

GILBERT & GEORGE, 1980

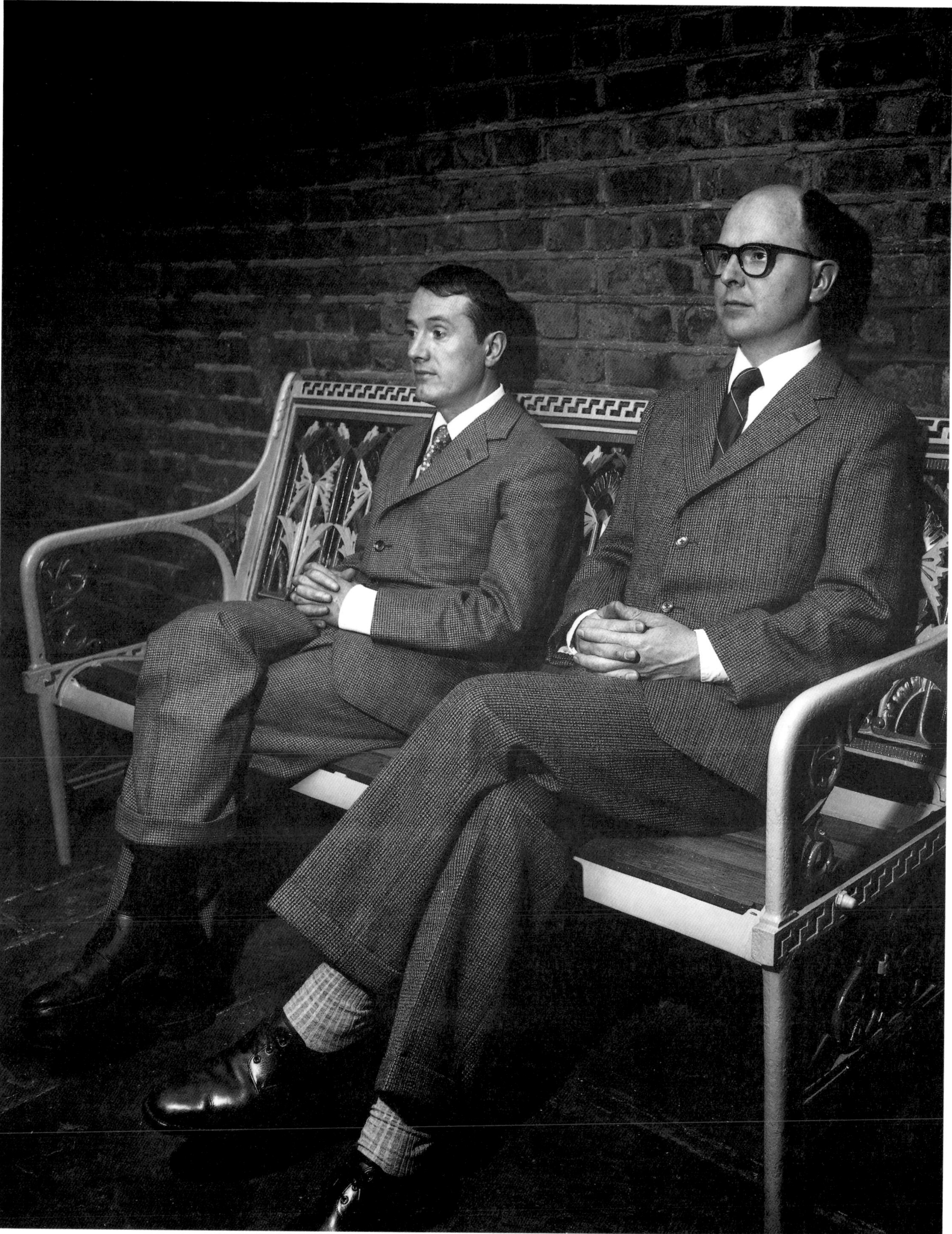

GALE
FURS
8 FOURNIER ST.
01-247 2014 / 5734
Dilal Fashions
Manufacturers of
LADIES · GENTS · CHILDRENS
SUEDE & LEATHER
GARMENTS

HELL.
death toll

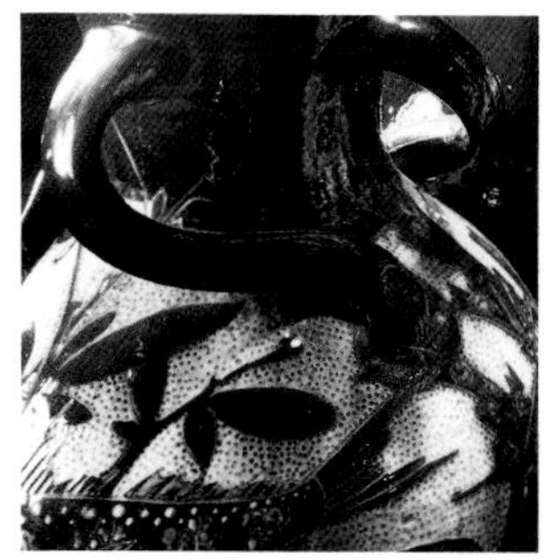
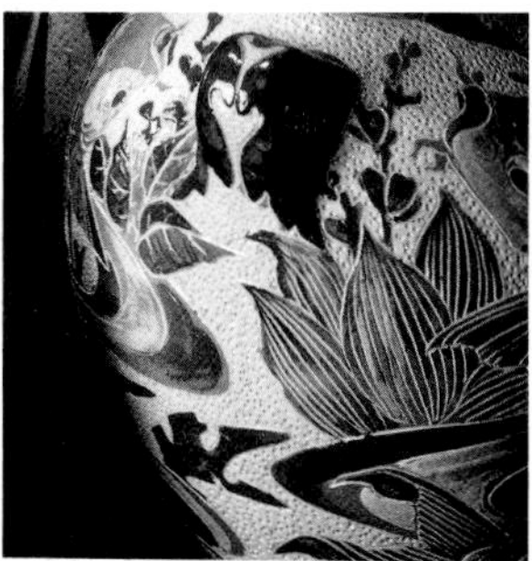
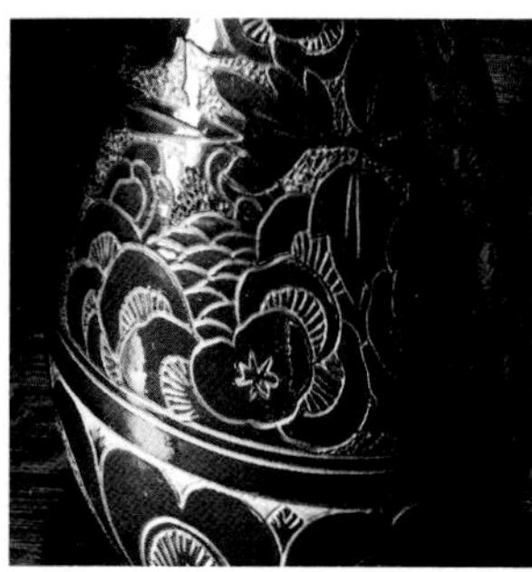

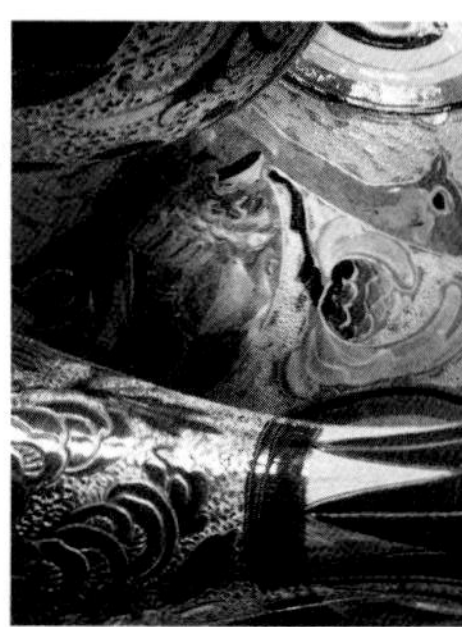

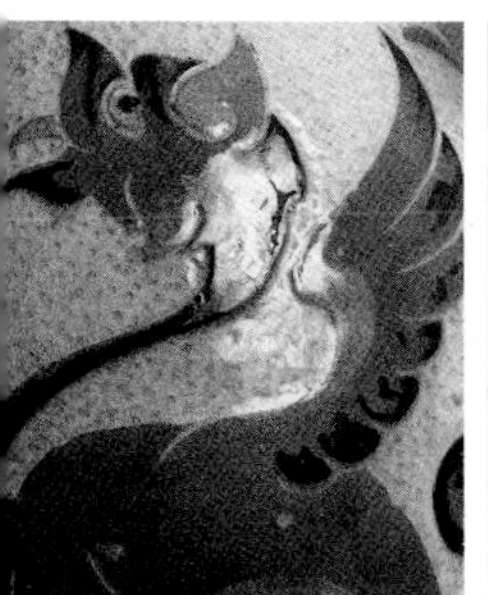

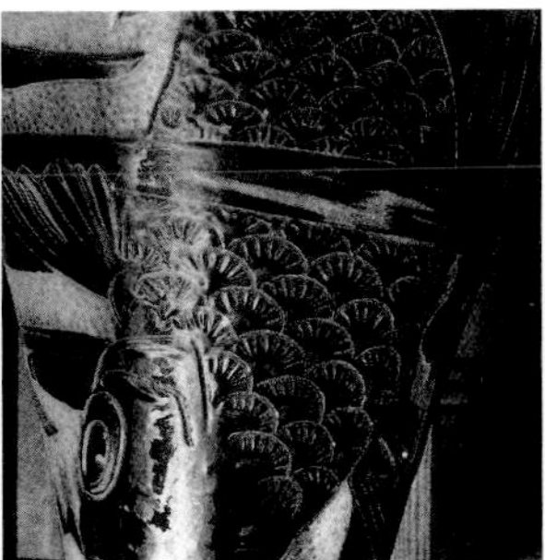

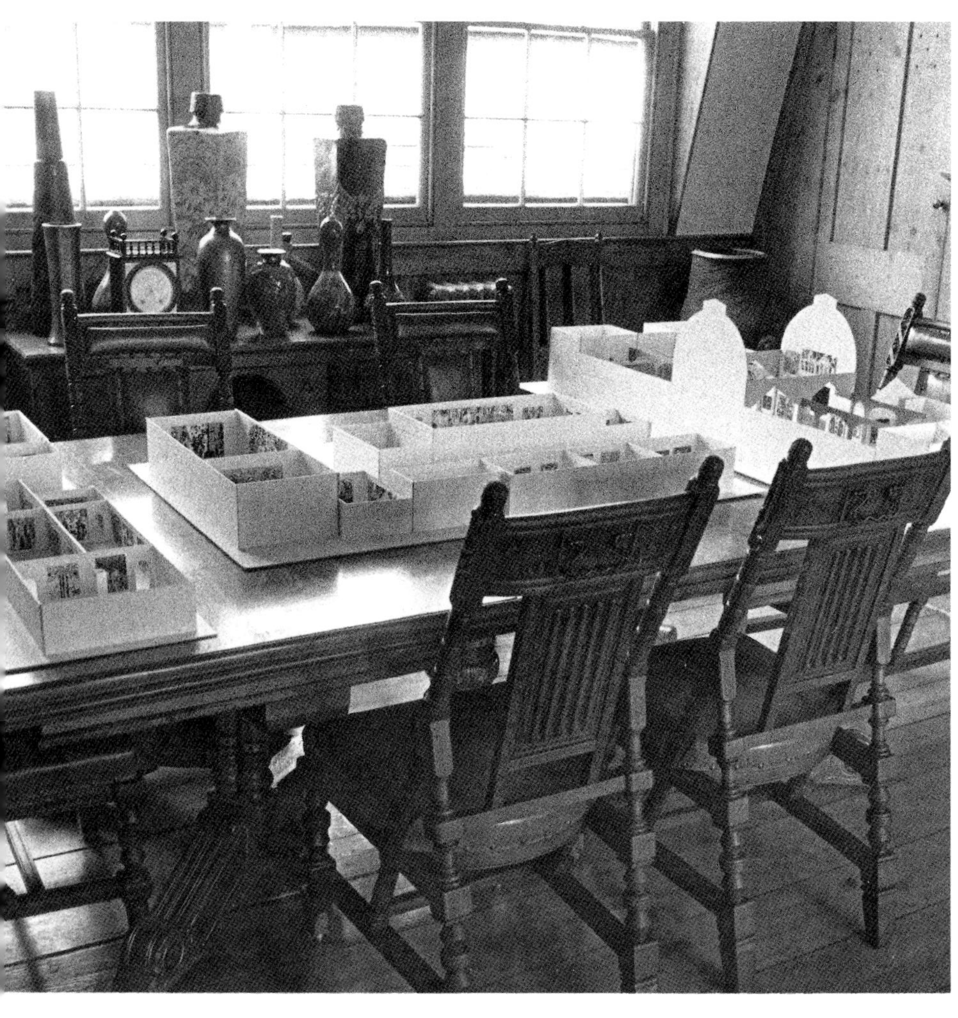

LIFE
1984

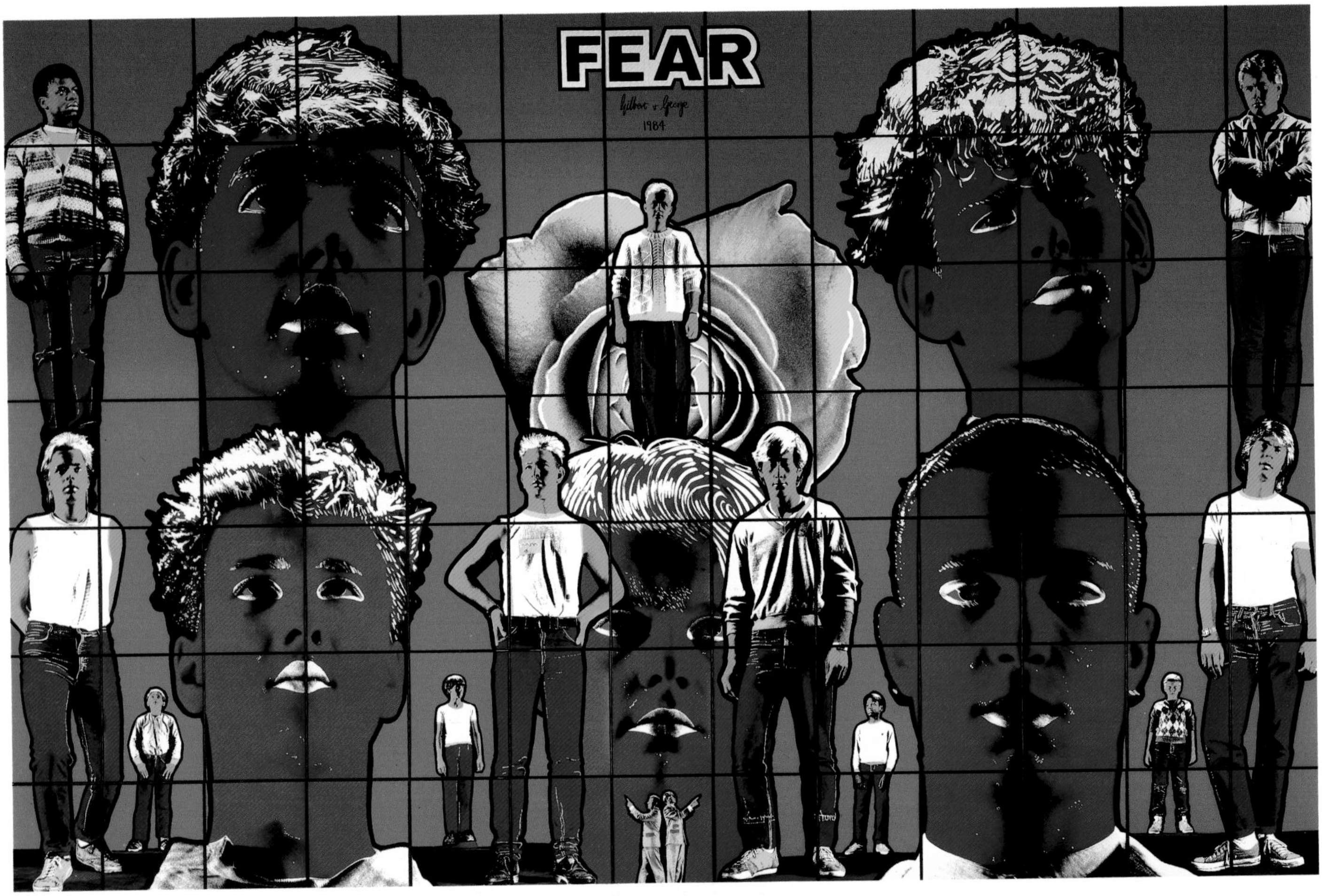

FEAR
1984

HOPE

DEATH

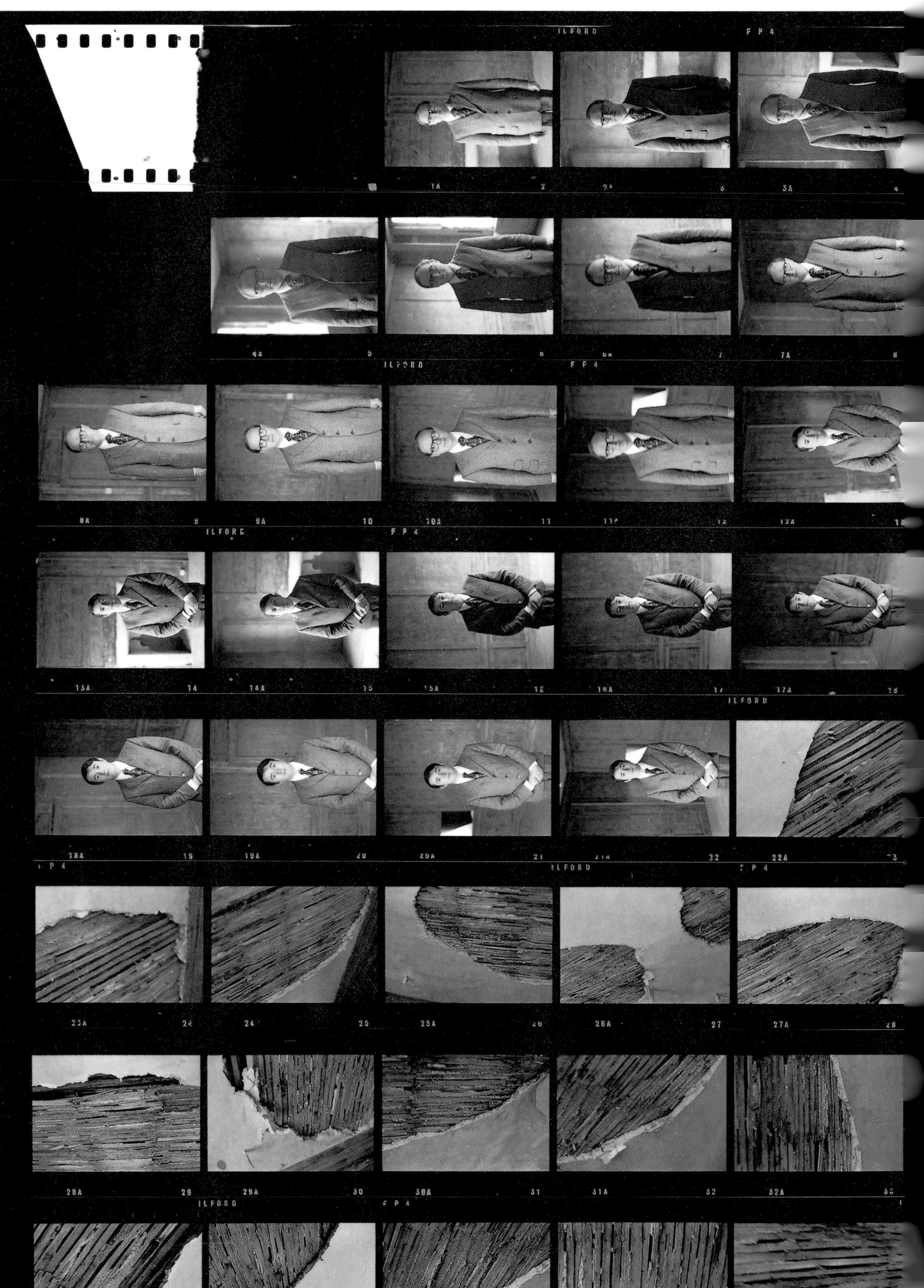

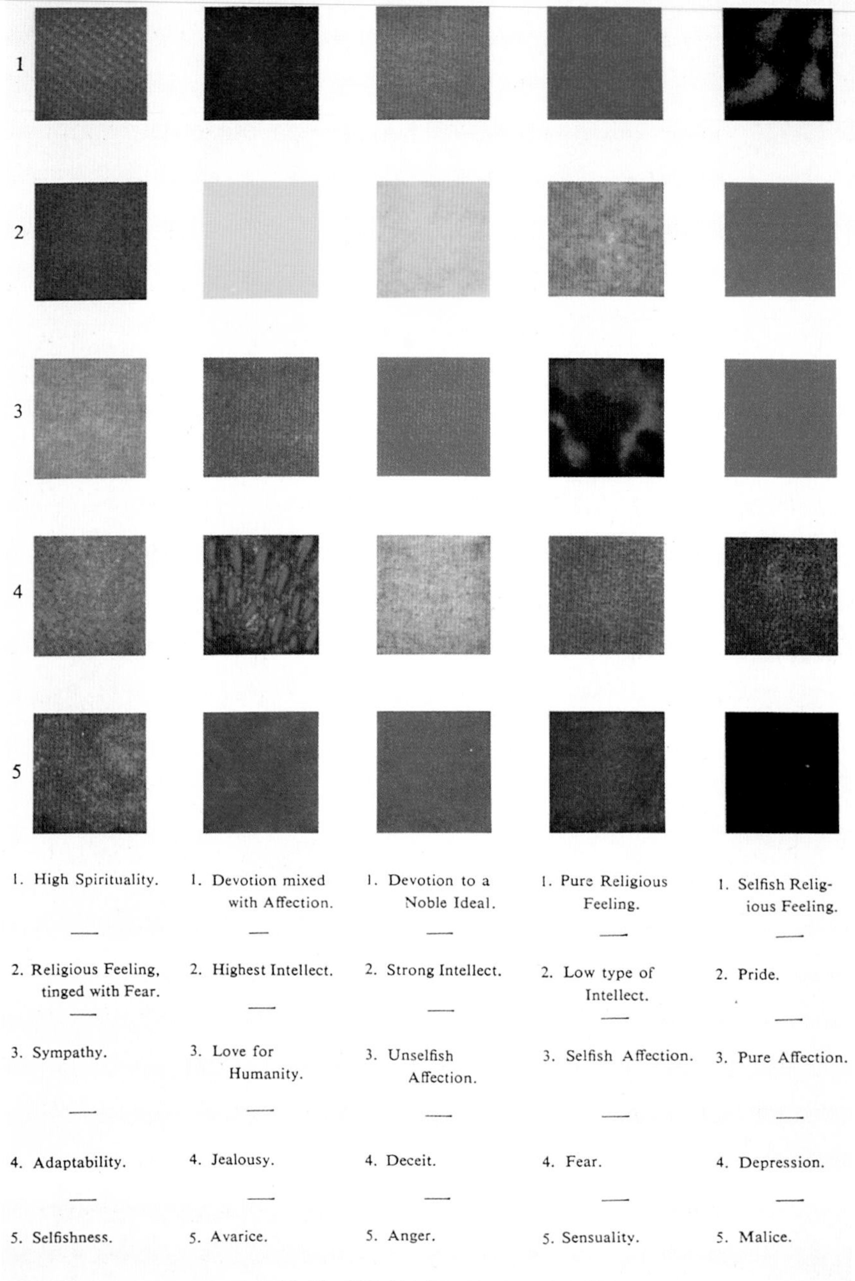

KEY TO THE MEANINGS OF COLOURS

Paola: There are many objects in your house, and they all seem to have so much presence. It's frightening in a way. George: Our vases should be frightening because all the vases that we collect are made or designed by people who were not interested in beauty, or shape, or form, but meaning. They were interested in making a vase which spoke to people; the same as in a poem, a composition, a concert, or a play—a work of art spoke to people. All of our vases are statements to people. They are human statements on the human condition. You could divide the designers into two groups: those who wanted to make a nice vase to look at and those who wanted to do something different. Elton, for instance. We're sitting surrounded now by Elton vases. Elton was anti-visual; he was anti-decoration. He hated it if someone said that they liked one of his vases. He didn't do them for liking; he did them for meaning—visual meaning—the eye as the way to the soul, to the heart, the head, and to the cock, to the sex. It's not just to the eye. It's an antique idea that visual art should be for the eye. It is a limited, twisted, awful understanding. Gilbert: The eye is the way to the true forces. Visual is foremost a religion of thought. George: Thought and feeling and dreads, hopes, fears—everything there is. Elton's vases are mainly covered with plant forms. Elton thought that every plant form, every form in nature that existed, was equal to a person: if it was an oak, or a dandelion, or whatever the plant was, it had a character much the same as a person had; it could live and express itself as equally as people. Gilbert: We are always looking for parallels to ourselves. Flowers are for us parallels. *How do you go about buying these vases? Do you always share exactly the same views?* George: It's very simple: we buy the vases that agree with us. It's not a question of which one Gilbert likes, which one George likes. We're not interested in that "individual" sort of idea. It's like a couple, or a company, or a marriage, or a king and queen, or....We support that idea. It's normal that every society is made up of couples, after all. Not complicity—we believe more in we. We don't believe it's a combination of two people. We believe it's what comes out of the two people. *Why the nineteenth century? Why the late nineteenth century?* Gilbert: In the nineteenth century the form was not abstract. The form was...to go inside yourself, to ask questions. And I think it was more near to our sort of art. It was more a philosophy for art than art as a form. And that is what we like most. George: Indeed, with the end of the nineteenth century came the collapse of so-called Christian culture in art. For I don't know how many hundreds of thousands of years people thought that art was good because art was telling people about goodness, which equalled Christianity or a social system. It was the lord of the manor, a picture of the lord of the manor with his dogs, or it was Jesus and his disciples. We didn't have "fine art." *What about all the art done for the church and the popes?* George: Yes, this was done for a purpose. The church arranged for pictures to explain the message. Gilbert: Well, I think we are doing unhappiness in his life. He stands in front of the picture; he will be speaking to it. There is friendship in that moment between the artist and the viewer. We don't believe that the art is just on the wall and that the artist is some kind of brutal person who says, "I was trying to say this in this picture, and if you don't get it bad luck." We don't believe that. Gilbert: No, we don't believe that at all. We feel we are in the forefront. We are trying to change moralities—in the forefront with everybody, not just elitist people—with everybody. George: We believe that art is political. When you vote, you vote not with your knowledge of politics, you vote with how you are culturally. If I say to you, "Dickens," whether or not you've read one single book of Dickens, something happens in your heart, and that, we say, is culture. And that is how you go to the polling stations; that is how you vote, in a free Western society. This is how political we think art is. Those books from the public libraries—or wherever—if you chuck them onto the street, nobody's going to read them all, are they? I mean, chuck all the Dickens books in the world onto the street so it becomes litter. Litter it's going to become—isn't it? Culture is the only force. Gilbert: It's a question of form and content. If you switch on the television and it says that war has broken out in some country, we don't want to know just that. We want to know who's been killed; what is the culture behind the war? I think there is an evolution of life, and we the artists always should be in the front...changing it. *You don't want to be assertive or direct about it, you want to be...contaminating?* Gilbert: Yes, behind the scenes. George: We are not telling, we are advising—we're recommending, we're suggesting. For instance, what we're saying is that, if someone comes to an exhibition of our work, and they stand in front of the picture, and they see a work called *Holy Hope* or *Death Faith,* or whatever the work is, whether they are opposed to the work or not, they have seen it, and, at that moment, we have a subversion. We are getting into the life of that person, and that is what we are interested in. *Like an illness?* Gilbert: Like a good illness. George: The cultural force, with people in a free society, in a Western democracy, has not been evaluated yet. It is enormous, I mean, around the corner is a church; on the next corner there is a bank; and we have a school; we have roads. We hope nobody will break into our house at this very moment because we have police. And it is all arranged by culture. It is a high ideal of order. We exist, we live, we possess through this sense of culture. *Do you like order?* George: Yes, we like order for progress and the betterment of mankind. We support that, very strongly. *But you said that you also like to be subversive.* George: Subversion is the form of progress. It is how progress is arranged. *How do you put together the idea of order and subversion?* George: The first school that was arranged was not arranged with total agreement. I'm sure that many people were against the idea of education for people. We always say that there is one sheet of paper you can take onto the street with a art that way, because we like to speak with our art. But they used to speak— George: They were speaking for the bishop and we're speaking for ourselves. *They were speaking for power.* George: Yes, they were commissioned, for the authority. And, with the collapse of that, artists became completely terrified—unlike ourselves—completely terrified. What should we do now? What do we do? We have no preface. And the only chance they thought they had was to become obscure and mystifying. So that the more strange you became, and the less people understood, the more refined, the better it was, they thought. So if they did a picture of the lord of the manor, and all of the servants swept past him with their brooms and their tea trays, not noticing the picture, then the lord of the manor was better, because he understood the picture; nobody else did. It was maintaining the power of the intellectual elite. And we don't believe in that. We believe that pictures are for the people, not just for people who understand Western art history, or cubism, or the history of whatever. Gilbert: The late nineteenth century—it's the flowering of modernity, all that we hope for now, I think it is because England in the nineteenth century was very powerful. The whole idea of modernity started here, I really believe that. Webb... Mackintosh...then you have the Viennese who copied from Mackintosh. We want to go back to that philosophy of life, and you could say in a way that this feeling was at the beginning of formalism too. *Form that brings you back to feelings?* Gilbert: It would be like feelings, yes...of being alive, of being like a flower, like a pig, etc. You know what I mean? We don't like aesthetic forms just for aesthetic reasons. George: Again, take Elton; the man who made these vases didn't want to be a potter. He just started one day. He dug some clay out. He didn't know what a kiln was. He had to build his own kiln, and then he realized he needed a person to help. He asked the local school—some small school in the country—if they had a school leaver, you know, a person just leaving school. And he was allowed to choose. And who did he choose? He chose a small boy with a hunchback. This deformed boy and Elton, a very grand person, with lots of money and things, worked together for forty years—twenty years in the last century, twenty years in this century. He bridged the centuries completely. And the hunchback boy died within the same year as Elton, presumably from a broken heart. Why else? So, for us, visual is not for the eye. We are against art for the eye. Art for the eye is a question of aesthetics and that supports the old regime; that is art as an entirely visual language, so that, if people don't understand what it is, sooner or later the curator of the museum will give them a small lecture and tell them what they are supposed to be looking at. We believe that art should be from the heart, should be a friendship between the viewer and the artwork. That is, the viewer comes to art, or to the museum or gallery, whatever it is, not with his knowledge of Western art history, but with his life—not with his knowledge of cubism, but with his every beating, every success, every failure, every happiness, every

sentence on it that everyone will sign: "There is room for improvement." Everyone will sign the sheet of paper. You can take it all over the world, and you'll get a million, billion, trillion signatures with that. But what I'm saying is if you wrote down one more thing than that, if you write down one suggestion, then you will find that some people will sign and some people won't. We as artists know what we believe in, and we recommend that in every work that we ever do, whether it be called *Life Without End* or *Drunk With God* or *Death Without Fear.* Gilbert: I think it's very important to build up a fortress around ourselves. We are building it up with thoughts, ideas that we really like, that are important to us. That's how we started to collect; we never thought about this stuff before. George: We started very late in our careers; before, we hated everything. Gilbert: And then we started to buy all this stuff. We always felt we were neglected artists. We always felt neglected because we were doing it here in England. George: What do you mean "we felt"? We *do* feel—the same today. Gilbert: Well, yes, anyway we did at the time we started, and so we thought we had to fortress ourselves to make ourselves more solid to fight the enemies. George: To put it in a most vulgar way, if you have a house, like we have, filled with these vases, you will still have people who will say, "I say, got any Lalique?" You will still have people like that, who don't understand one single vase in the house. They are just looking to see whether we have the vases that are popularly known in the color supplements. And that same person is the person who will be unaware of contemporary life, contemporary feeling. See, we are fighting for a heritage in a way. *So, what are the enemies?* George: The enemy is the unthinking, unfeeling, unsexing person. *From what you say, I get a great feeling of rigidity, but, at the same time, you're not rigid at all.* Gilbert: Give us a chance, hang on. (laughter) George: Well, we're quite rigid in our rules, yeah. Gilbert: We are rigid because I think we have...we have a naive idea in which we believe, and we like that, and we don't...we don't want to be sophisticated people that are all liberal in all different ways. We have a clear idea, a simple idea of what is good, and that's what we do. George: Thrust..."liberal" means bended, elastic: thinking this, this other thing—seeing everyone's point of view. I remember at one of our earliest interviews we said that "we are happily narrow-minded." We like to be narrow-minded. Broad-minded people didn't achieve so much as far as we can see, historically—not so much. They always saw so many people's point of view that they didn't do anything in the end. *Your feelings are the opposite of rigidity.* George: Well, it's very good from one point of view in that we are able to make works that speak to a wide range of people. Gilbert: Yes. That's because we are very interested in being normal people who react to the world. And that's why our public is very big—because we are like them. *How do people react to your work?* George: People never say, "I like your stuff." I remember we were in Baltimore and were just taking one last look at the exhibition. We were on the way to the airport and a young man came up to us and asked us if we would sign a copy of the catalogue. We signed it and I thought he would disappear immediately. But then he said, "Do you mind if I say something to you?" And we said, "Of course not, certainly." And he said, "I'd like to tell you how comfortable I feel sitting in front of *Naked Love*." And his eyes were completely *filled with tears*. He didn't say, "I love your picture, I love your painting," or something. He just went immediately to the meaning, what we wanted. To put it more accurately, we should tell the story from Palm Beach. This extremely elderly person came to us at an opening. It was a great party and everyone's riotously enjoying their drinks and they're making brawls and looking at the exhibition things and then this very, very elderly gentleman came up to us on two sticks and said, "I enjoy this exhibition and I'll tell you why." We said, "Why?" He said, "It sure scared the hell out of me." It's amazing. Gilbert: I only know one artist who did that, Caravaggio. That he was pained, that's nothing. But his ideas were of what life was all about. You must open your eyes completely in front of the picture. George: And *then* the picture will speak to you. That is why we're opposed to the tradition of the profession of fine arts. Gilbert: In the twelfth century, they did these big murals, but people didn't know it was art; it was figures in front of them, speaking to them. And that's what we like to do. We like to speak about modern living and not about art. And that's why we believe modern art is the most exciting. I don't like to go to see old churches and all that stuff. I only like modern art. *Did you always think this way?* Gilbert: I think it is through what we have started to do. George: Yes, we became more and more conscious of our balance; we developed a sense of balance, we would say. I think we were quite naive when we started. We had this idea to do living sculpture, and it was very good because we were *living* and trying to speak to people. That is what we're still doing. It's very good because every other artist has to go in the studio and start to paint, and we don't do that. We have to have our ideas. And I think it was at that point, the most innovative part of our career, when we said that *we were* the art. *When did you two meet each other?* George: 1967. *What were you both doing?* Gilbert: Art, art, art. George: We were doing it separately. (laughter) And we've been doing it together ever since. *When did you, Gilbert, start doing art?* Gilbert: I went to art school in Italy. *And where did you meet?* Gilbert: We met at college; we went to St. Martin's. George: I think the most important point for our work was when we left

the school and we were left with ourselves. That is when we started saying that we were the art and started doing the living sculpture. And that is what we are still doing. I think that was the most inventive part. Gilbert: Yes, I think that was the biggest evolution for us. *You told me that you were a boy from the...* Gilbert: Middle Ages. (laughs) *Yes, and also West England, and that you grew up in a small town. And I asked you how come you had such a good accent, such a proper accent. And you told me this story...* George: Very simple. My mother was a very snobbish, high-minded person, who had the right idea of it. She was interested in betterment and advancement. Therefore she sent me to elocution lessons. Myself and my brother—we went to elocution lessons. The fact that the elocution master tried to seduce us was beside the point. My mother's idea was good, though. *You told me that she kept you isolated from everyone else.* George: Entirely, entirely. *Didn't have any interactions with the people in the town, in the village, as a child?* George: Absolutely none. I wasn't even allowed to say, for instance, the words "father" or "dad" or "daddy," or anything to do with the masculine side. It was completely taboo in the family. I was brought up without those words. *Did you have a father?* George: No. He disappeared just before I was born, I imagine. But I was not allowed to say that. We were totally in a woman's world. *And how did the elocution lessons work?* George: "How now, brown cow, eating the green, green grass." (laughs) "Around the ragged rocks the rugged rascal ran." Things like that, you know. "Peter Piper picked a peck of pickled peppers." Things like that. The moment we learned to pronounce all the lessons correctly we had to progress downwards to the half-landing of the stairs and recite them from there. And then we had to learn them all again. It took ages and ages of course to get them completely correct from there. And then he said, "Lower." So we went down to the first landing. It was "how now, brown cow, eating the green, green grass" until we got to the bottom of the building and he thought we'd passed out as ideal English people. But he was a dirty old man as well. I remember him telling us that he'd been in the navy as a young person and his introduction to the navy had been that they'd painted his cock blue as part of the initiation ceremony—and then the conversation that evening went on from there. *How did you react?* George: I was rather impressed. Rather impressed. There is only one force left amongst people and that is culture—the only force that's left to mankind. Gilbert: But, you know, the biggest force is existence. And nobody knows what life is all about. You only know that aside from ourselves there is a part everyone wants

to play and it is a kind of existence—force. George: If there is any inspiration that we ever had in our life, *if* there *is*—there is hardly an artist who has ever had *any*—our inspiration would be the realization of the individual person existing on the planet earth, that at the same time as we are thinking some idiotic thought, about what we are going to do today, or tomorrow, about art or not art, or things we have talked about previously—at the same time there are all these people all around our planet. That's what we love most—that there are artists, and there are Germans, and then there are Zulu-Germans. It's an amazing idea. Amazing. We love the idea, not of people, but of every single individual—not groups, but of every single person. We continue to include ourselves in the pictures because we want to constantly remind people that *we're* saying something to them. We don't believe that art should be reassuring. Most art is reassuring, you know. We believe that it should be threatening and should have to do with change, not reassurance, because change is what we are interested in. Gilbert: We like the order because we need it; on the other side, we like a disorder to free ourselves and make for new ideas. We are the disorder because that's a very important part. *There is a young poet, David Robilliard, whose work you are interested in publishing, but who is so self-destructive and feels so threatened by any achievement that you had to fight with him in order to publish his first book. But, you were very taken with his destructiveness.* George: We are interested in destructiveness. We see that in people, we see that in groups of people, we see that in cities, we see that in nations, we see it worldwide. *And you think that sometimes destructiveness can be a germ for...* George: It can be a force for people—"people" meaning non-artists. We have different centers; we are not normal people in that way. We see life based on three equal forces: the brain (or the head), then the soul, and the sex. And we say that every single thing that people do, think, say, fear, dread is based on a combination of those three elements. You're always working between those three elements. Gilbert: Some use more sex, some more brain, some more heart. George: It's always a combination, always. There is nothing else. We went on this trip with a friend in Thailand. There are so many male brothels there. We would go there and they would ask us to choose and there would be all these boys lined up. And we always used to say, "It doesn't matter, the first one." I wouldn't like to say, "That one isn't suitable," and see other people's faces drop. That must be a disaster, isn't it? To be not chosen. So we said, "Anyone is fine; they're all fantastic; it doesn't matter which one." But our friend was always choosing. He was so choosy that a selection was never possible. He actually chose one one evening, then went back to the hotel, and then he changed his mind: "I don't think this *is* the right one." So he took him back to get his money back. Can you imagine anything more embarrassing? Can you imagine the poor tart? He must have been so unhappy; it's cruel. So we always said, "It's rude to choose." His only interest, then, was in one particular barman at the hotel. And, of all the people in the whole of Thailand, anyone could have been able to tell him that this was not the suitable one. He was probably the only heterosexual barman in the whole of Thailand, and that's the one he wanted. Only that one would do. He was even rather ugly. He wasn't interesting or anything. But he had to have that one. So he planned and worked all week. The last evening, he managed to get a date with this boy. They went out to dinner; then they went to a club. Then the young man took him to a brothel—with girls. He didn't speak much English. He didn't understand what our friend wanted. So then they ended up in a room with fifteen girls to choose from. Our friend said, "I don't want *them;* I want *you*!" Perhaps the boy still didn't understand. He was saying, "Which one?" And then our friend's plane was about to leave. By this time he was so worried about his plane leaving in four hours, you know, and he didn't know how to get out. He was saying, "Well, I have to go." And the boy was saying, "Which girl?" So, to get out, he just did this girl, just in order to escape. And in that moment he got syphilis. Gilbert: And the girl told him off because he came; you're not allowed to come into them! George: Apparently it's very dangerous. We went straight back to the clinic when we came back. And we were completely clean—perfect. Our friend had green syphilis. It's a story that really tells a lot. *How do you see sex?* George: How do we see sex? My God, it's as dreadful as anything else! We have a big interest, a big interest...not shagging or something—we are not so interested in that—but in more particular forms, anything amusing really. I think sex is more interesting for amusement. I think it is more interesting when it has to do with everything—with life, with people and places—rather than pure sex. Gilbert: I think our art is very sexy. We love to do very sexy pieces—not that they just look sexy, but that they have the feeling of sexuality as well. We say that the sexuality in our work is not our sexuality. It is the relationship between what we are saying and the viewer. Because we say that a person should come in front of a picture with their life. We believe that the artist should have a realization of the gift of life, and the only thing you can do if you understand that is to do something in exchange for it. At least you have to give something back. That's why we say, ideally, the artist is the giver. He's like a public servant, in a way. George: We're more interested in the viewer, really. We do it for the viewer, not for ourselves. Gilbert: And we never change our minds. I think that's very important. We accept everything that we do. We would never say, "That's not good enough." George: They're always taken from our existence. We never think of a piece to do, or...we never think, "Shall we do a piece with a mountain?" "Shall we do a piece with a tree?" How we are, we do that. So there's no decision for us to make, except in how we are in our heads, or our hearts, or our sex, or our life, or in our thoughts, or in our fears—that's what we do. We just lift it from our knowledge and existence and love—whatever. Gilbert: And we never change; we never change. George: They're like printed off—printed off from ourselves. As the design is, so is the finished piece. It never changes in between. We just fall together, from our lives. We don't do what Gilbert thinks or feels, or what I feel or think. We do what we feel. It's from ourselves, the combined view. Gilbert: Often you keep chucking together—that's a composition, no? Because we are going out and take photographs of exactly what we feel that year, we can expect to be all right. All that we are feeling must be right. So we just chuck it together. It doesn't matter how it is, if it's more this way, more that way. George: These are the contacts. We both take the photographs—very fast. They're an enormous session. You see, there are just pages and pages. We think photography is a better medium. It's like sketching, you know? You can just do it exactly. And it is completely beautiful, like a person is. A hand is a hand, a face is a face. It doesn't look like eccentric, freaky twentieth-century art, which is what we dislike so much. There's this big tradition where everything has to look (makes a retching sound) strange—it's something that infuriates the lower classes. Modern art—we don't believe in that. We believe in art that is true to life. Gilbert: We prefer to infuriate them with real people. George: Yes—with a message, not with a form. So not true-to-life in a physical way because there are always elements that were never together in real life. If there are six people in a picture, the people probably never met each other, let alone stood together. They're artificially constructed. Gilbert: It's all artificially done; that's what we like. You can make a flower like a person and all that stuff. But we have a bank of images, we have an alphabet. Every year, we go out, or in the studio, to take images that we like—ten or fifteen thousand images. From that stuff we can compose our work. It's very interesting because we never have anything in our studio, nothing. We never see what we are doing because we always do it in the darkroom. Only when it's completely finished, then we see it. George: Generally at the moment of exhibition, in fact. We are never working on it; they're never up to be worked on, as an artist has them in a studio. We work on them in detail. The whole, finished work we only see at the moment of exhibition. We work blind. Gilbert: We just use our thought and imagination. Then you see it in the end. We just do the testing. Every figure we are testing for the right darkness. George: And the gold leaf and the colors are added afterwards. Gilbert: It's all hand-done, all hand-done. We mix our own colors. We have formulas; we use photographic dye. *And what is the passage in your work between black and white and the colors.* George: We started in black and white. Then we wanted to include an aggressive color and that's red

Gilbert: An underlining of the feeling. George: Many people didn't know how we did it, technically. It's all based on a black-and-white photograph and superimposing one after another, like building up a picture, superimposing the color and the figures. Gilbert: It's a technique that we developed very slowly; we didn't know anything about it. We invented it. Our systems, our colors and all that, we just did it, very slowly. George: Yellow is for other people. Red is for ourselves. (looks through photos) Gilbert: You see, green is for nature. This is a cabbage. George: It looks like a flower...*or a brain.*

Francesco Clemente

pelu peluzzu
che mè refole e viento
t'ha purtato
dimme, aro' si nato?
ngoppa a nu' cazzo duro e nu surdato?
o ngoppa na pepella verginella e nè zitelle?
o pilu nun rispunne
oh, pel'i culo si allora!

di Giacomo (?)

e quanno good good
chiù blacker da midnite
nun pote camme

(1945?)

when the echo falls
one will dismiss it
when it calls again
one will miss
it falling in love with the present
while one is able of it
when the shadows enlarge will one
enter it or stay where
he is now, what will one do, how

JOHN WIENERS

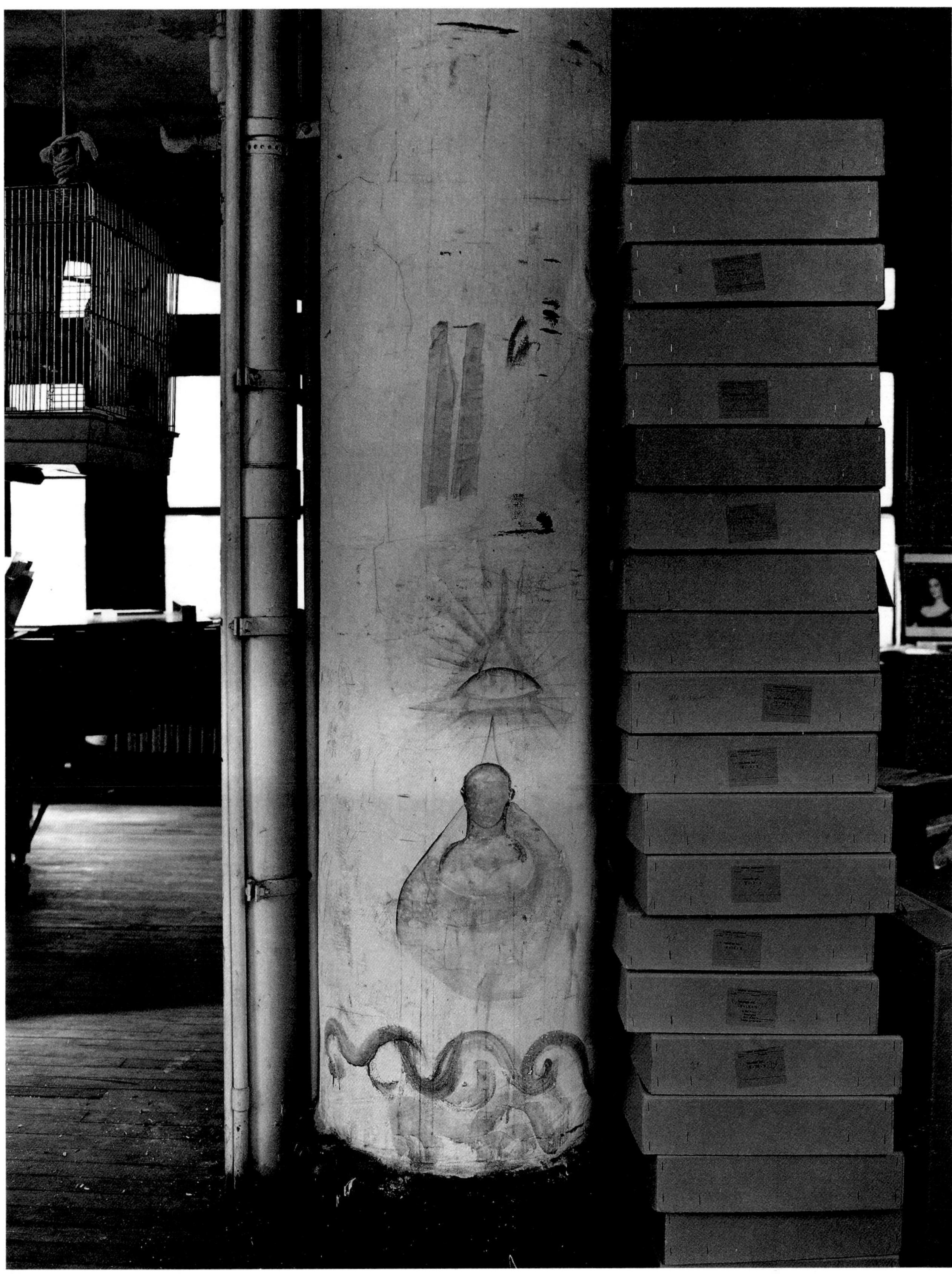

PIU MI SENTIVO
ADORAVO
UNA PRIGIONE
IL CIELO O IL MARE
ERA LA

POLVO ESPECIAL
Uselo polveándose

Legitimo Polvo
DE ABRECAMINO
ORO Y PLATA
OFRECIMIENTO
CHANGO MACHO
ESPIRITU DE LA BUENA SUERTE

LEGITIMO POLVO
AMARRADOR
CONSIGUE SU DESEO
USELO/POLVEANDOSE

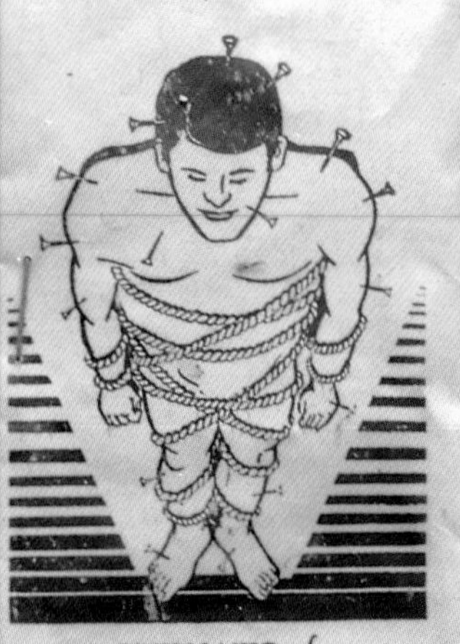
Te Tengo Amarrado
y Claveteado

POLVO MISTICO
Toloache
USELO POLVEANDOSE
ES MUY EFECTIVO

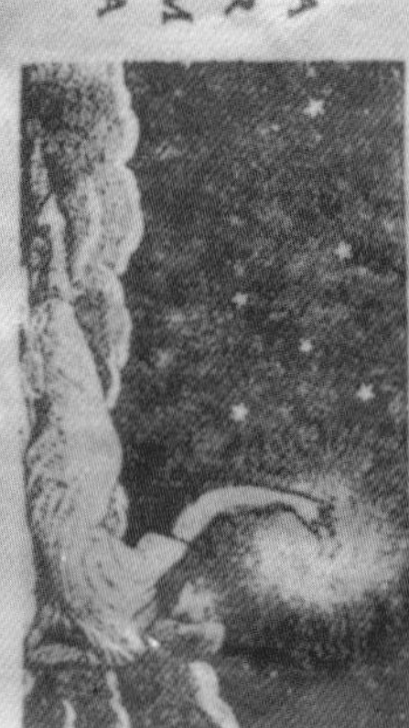
ARMA
POLVO
CONTRA LIGADURA ASTRAL
PODEROSA

POLVO ESPECIAL
TRIANGULO MAGICO
Corta Trabajo Negro. Acostumbre usarlo polveándose todo el cuerpo diariamente de Luna Creciente a Luna Llena. Este polvo es muy especial para retirar
clase de maleficios y males

POLVO LEGITIMO
TENTACION DE AMOR

LEGITIMO POLVO
YO DOMINO A MI
MUJER

LEGITIMO POLVO DE
San Ignacio
de Loyola

LEGITIMOS POLVOS
"YO DOMINO A MI HOMBRE

POLVO DE LA
BRUJA
CONTRA MALEFICIOS

Paola: Now that your family has moved upstairs, this floor of the house is slowly being reclaimed by your studio; it still has the structure of a family space but the functions have changed: the myna bird, sitting in its big cage in the middle of the kitchen table, four tomes of Thomas Aquinas next to it, the children's bedroom has become a little cell for drawing, the corner room with the window on Broadway is barred off by cardboard, an ominous black typewriter sits in the corridor, over it on the wall hang various photographs like little poems, files with the writings and poetry published by Hanuman Books are heaped on a table. The Hanuman Books, these little books of poetry and writings that fit in the palm of the hand that you and Raymond Foye publish in India, how did they start? They remind me of the books of drawings you used to make years ago. Francesco: Yes, that's where they come from. My first book with Kalakshetra was in 1977, the little book with the red cover and the cards inside; then Raymond came over to see me in India in 1985, and he fell in love with this mistake-filled technique of Indian printing. So he decided to produce these books and asked me to be the co-editor. The idea immediately tickled my vanity and curiosity. *You choose the manuscripts together, don't you?* Yes, there are two veins: one is contemporary poems—that comes from Raymond—and the other is these "wrong" European mystics of the thirties—Daumal, Michaux, Simone Weil—that comes more from my taste. *Raymond told me that the Indian printer wanted to censor one of the manuscripts you sent.* It was *Fuck Journal*. You know, at the printers in India they print Montessori books, various other edifying books, and in effect *Fuck Journal* was a bit of a problem for them. Here it is. It's sort of a phone book list, a monthly calendar of the activities of the writer Bob Flanagan with a dominatrix. *Raymond Foye, while persuading the printer not to censor the material, mentioned to him the erotic symbols on many Hindu temples. The printer finally gave in, but for him those erotic temple images were another thing.* And they're not another thing; it's the same thing...only they haven't realized it. (Reading from *Fuck Journal)* "She has sympathy for my hard on"...(laughs)... sympathy! *You often speak about this lightness that you find both in India and New York; in New York it's produced by this mixture of pressure and*

generosity. What is this lightness? It's like road signals; I have all these ideas in my head of directions I want to take—I can't do anything unless I think it's going to take me somewhere—but they are imaginary places and also imaginary categories. *What is it you like about New York, because you do like living here don't you?* I like living anywhere; it depends on how the day goes. New York is the end of the world, literally, where the world ends: it's the bottom of the sink, at the edge of the drain, where all the grunge deposits, the contrary of the center. It's the rim. *What is the most beautiful thing that happened to you last year in New York? (laughs)...* It didn't happen in New York; it happened in Philadelphia. I had lunch and spent a whole afternoon with the Indologist and author Stella Kramrisch, a person I have always admired. She had a beautiful sculpture which I imagine is a bust of Shiva, but I'm not sure. She picked up this standing lamp and leaned against the wall oscillating—moving this light back and forth so I could see all the shadows on the sculpture, so I could see it completely. *You mentioned the other day that a cactus suddenly bloomed in your midtown hotel room where you work and then a dragonfly came into the room...* There is no story; I came in the room one morning and the cactus had this incredible single bloom: deep, deep black, the most beautiful black—only it wasn't black, it was blue. A dragonfly come in through the open window a few days later to die in my room. I kept both. So now I have these two mummies... *Lately you seem to be thinking a lot about loss and death; these last paintings are called "Funerary Paintings" but they have the feeling of going through to another state of life.* The Funerary Paintings are not about physical death; they are about the death of the persona and what happens next. It's really just asking the question: is it possible to think about something else sometimes? *They remind me of the painting "Purgatory" you did years ago.* Yes, there is that, and also there is a painting I made about Central Park, a very long, long painting. It was called *Hortis Conclusis* and was a map of Central Park with a portrait of my daughter next to it...Funerary Paintings...there is really nothing I can say about them. *During one of your first visits to India you stayed with a guru and his disciples, and there you had this powerful realization that you were a painter and that that was your way of relating to the world, was the way you were going to express whatever you needed to express, to go through*

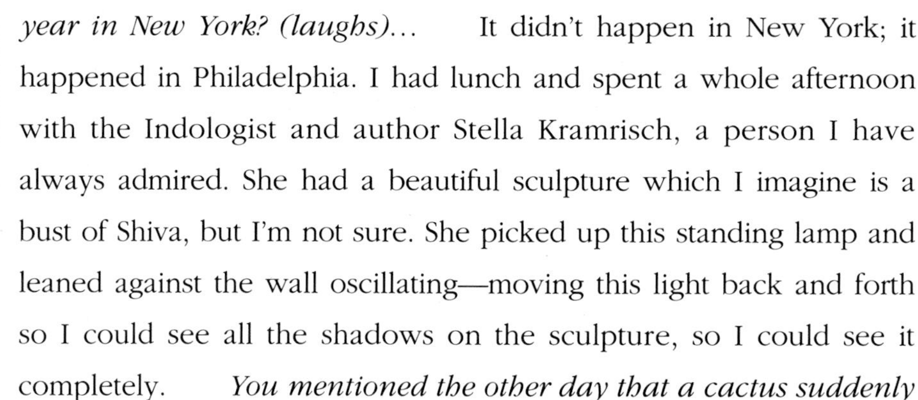

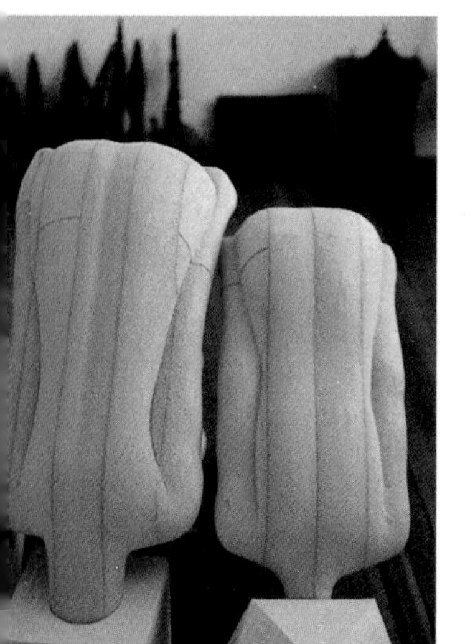

BUT, DESPITE THE DEATH OF THE BODY, I CAN STILL FEEL THE FULL FORCE OF MY BEING. I CAN EVEN HEAR A VOICE SPEAKING WITHIN ME. WHO IS THIS INSIDE ME? IT IS THE "I"—MY TRUE "I".

SO THIS "I" EXISTS APART FROM THE BODY. THEREFORE, "I" AM THE SPIRIT, WHICH IS IMMORTAL, DEATHLESS.

THEN THE BLOOD FLOWED THROUGH HIS LIMBS AGAIN AND HE BEGAN TO BREATHE. THE DEATH EXPERIENCE WAS OVER.

BUT DURING THAT INTENSE HALF-HOUR, THE PLAYFUL YOUNG SCHOOLBOY HAD ATTAINED REALISATION OF THE TRUE "I".

NOTHING COULD BE THE SAME AGAIN FOR VENKATARAMAN. EVERYONE NOTICED THE DIFFERENCE IN HIM.
I HAVE MADE YOUR FAVOURITE DISH AND YOU HAVEN'T TOUCHED IT. DON'T YOU WANT IT?
YES...

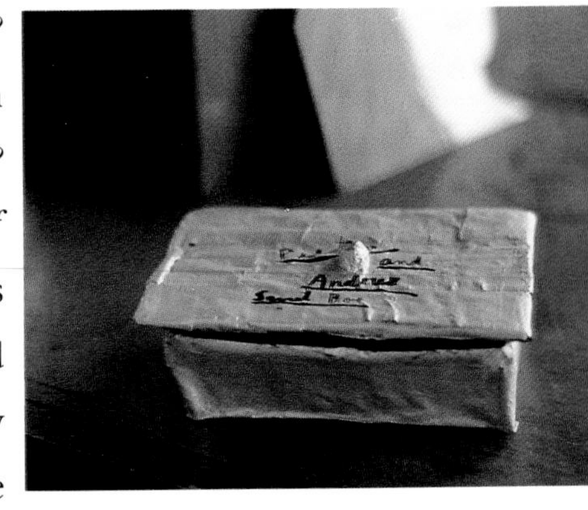

it to another stage. Are these paintings a development of that? They are tools; everything I do I see as a tool, as things you can use...in an itinerary. *And where does the itinerary lead to?* Somewhere else. *You are an intellectual who is distrustful of thought. Was this lack of trust always there?* My distrustfulness is a little older than me and my story. One of my favorite tales in the old Indian books is how they explain why we should not lie. They say that we should not lie because lying is the root of speech, so if we lie we expose the root of the tree of speech, and the tree is going to dry up. Is this pessimism? I don't know what it is. *In your painting, especially before the last body of work, you have always tried to keep as open a panorama as possible, including everything in the picture. You do that also in your life and with your little "schools of life"—groups of small objects you have in your studio.* Blake called Satan "the Unprolific" and I think what characterizes my attitude towards the work is the fact that I don't consider the world rich as most people do today; I consider it extremely poor. I think it is the poorest world since the beginning of history...the poorest. *You don't seem to be habitual. Do you have habits?* I spend all my day trying not to think of myself, not to talk about myself, not to start sentences with "I," nor thoughts. Naturally I fail miserably. At least I have reached the age where I know that all that I know is that I don't know, and all that I don't know is what counts and what I know doesn't count. So whatever I would tell you about my habits would be a lie, because it would be what I believe it is but which is really the negative of what it is, like the negative of a photograph. *For this book you wanted to add two of your recipes, the best Italian and Indian. What could be more everyday than that?* Yes, and we'll put in Di Giacomo's poem. *Yes, Di Giacomo's poem, and written underneath it: "Try and find a metaphysical key to this one!"* Di Giacomo's poem...to discourage the devout of the New Age in their search for spirituality...gratuitous spirituality. *(looking at some photos on the wall) Is this your daughter Chiara dressed and made up like an Indian dancer? For the first time, I see something of your wife Alba in her.* Yes, it is Chiara. I've always had this theory worked out that Chiara was very much like myself, while Nina I saw as very much like Alba, and I thought I was indulgent with Nina as I would be with Alba. Only recently I realized that, in fact, it's the opposite. Chiara is the one who is like Alba. I let Nina do anything she wants because she is like me. I am as totally indulgent with her as I am with myself.

Sigmar Polke

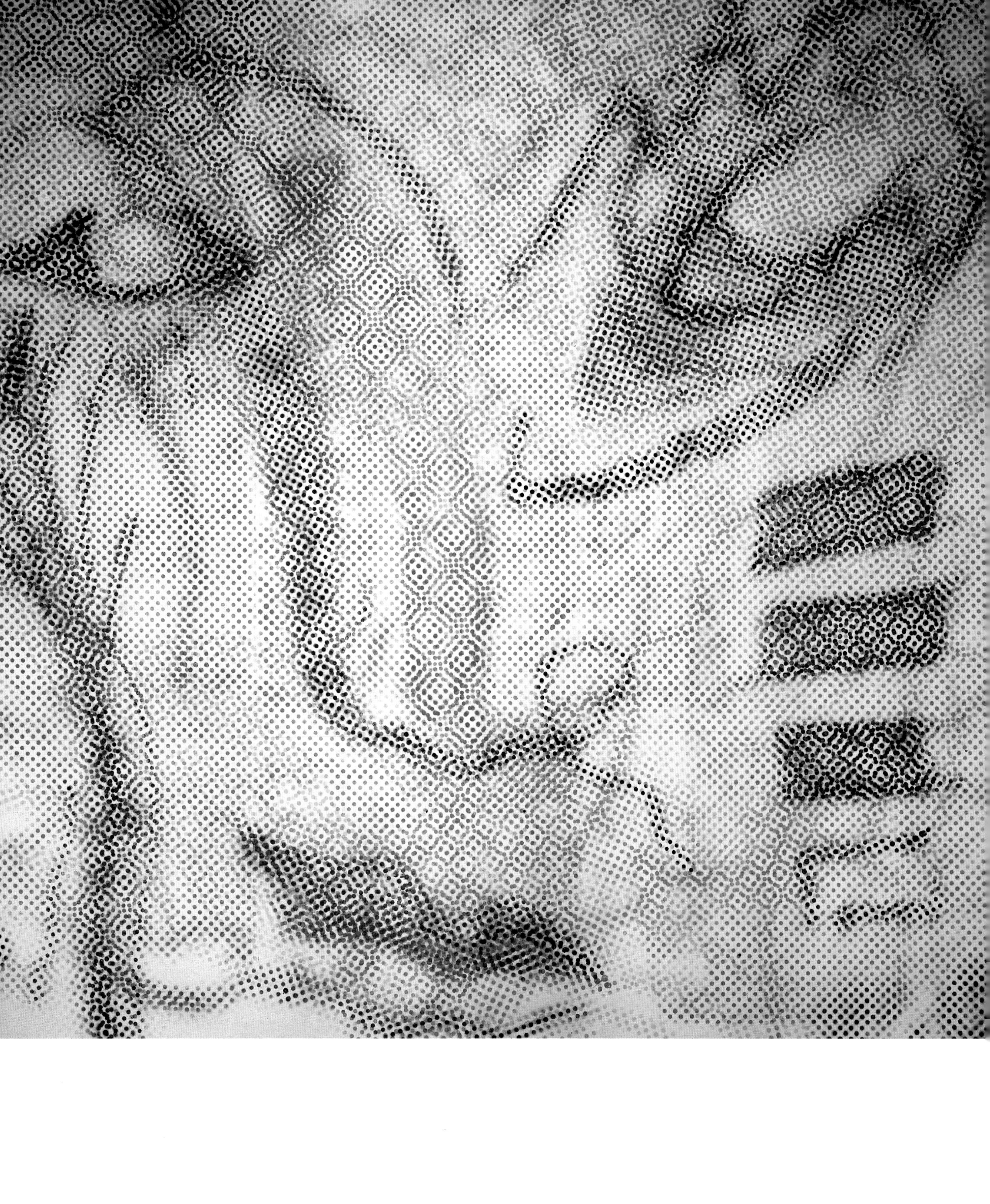

DAILY TRANSMUTATIONS

You pass through a courtyard and an exposed convent garden and ring a bell with someone else's name on it. If Sigmar is in, his full figure stands at the tall window (no windowsill, just a bar across it), and signals you to come up. The large rectangular room, windows on all sides, ends in a long hallway bathroom; an open narrow balcony takes you to another parallel room that looks like a gigantic garbage bin but is, in fact, something between a studio and a railway station's baggage room, the baggage being: an open wardrobe full of clothes, photos of healers cataloguing their 62nd fascicle of miracles, a collection of canary glass with an ultraviolet light next to it, etc...The next room: large rectangular windows on both sides; roofs, tree-tops and the steeples of the Cologne cathedral. The tree in the courtyard is Ailanthus; tree of heaven in China—trash-tree in New York. It's in flower now; the flowers smell sticky and good the first few days, and like cat's spray when they wither. Various contiguous piles of newspapers in the corner of the room. READING THE NEWSPAPER, ONE OF HIS IMPORTANT EVERYDAY ACTIVITIES—SO MANY LAYERS IN THOSE TITLES LINES WORDS. They are cut out, used in all sorts of other contexts; the different layers are physically repeated through the work. Drawings...HUMOR... another vehicle across reality. Photos from the newspapers are photographed, and rephotographed, enlarged projected painted on...you go through layer upon layer—end up in an altered reality, the image becomes a landscape you can traverse. TRANSMUTATIONS—things shed their skin and become other things through a process. PLANTS—the most extreme examples of transmutation—you DRINK or chew or swallow the juice of this plant (mandrake) and you rise from the dead and enter heaven—(bible)...REALITY. Is heaven always there? "Reality is an illusion created by the lack of alcohol!"—"Our holes are small and we shrink them more and more as we have to choose and construct." Some substances and some states of mind lead

NATURAL MINERAL WATER
Taste the mountain freshness
Bottled at source · Auvergne · France

to those inner doors. INTERACTION AND CHANCE. Sigmar has a collection of newspaper errors, cut-outs of errors enlarged and enlarged again. The context of the errors always gives another sense to it, and the actual error, amplified, has very particular shapes. INTERACTION AND THE HAPHAZARD. The mouse in his studio created a nest out of Sigmar's newspaper cut-outs; it was a very poetic nest—Sigmar photographed it—I never saw the photo. Sigmar paints some paintings with chemicals and minerals: silver nitrate, radium...the brush stroke or the splash of the material is there, but then the nitrate has its own LIFE, takes its own course—the sun, the light, the humidity, the time, scan its inner rhythm. RHYTHM... INSTRUMENTS. There are musical instruments in the room and in the studio; a hollow wooden pig from Papua that you beat on...a big gong from Java....He would like to have them in different rooms, in his wife Britta's room, at the museum, in the studio, and whoever feels like it plays them; the beginning of complex disciplines...a percussor and a thing to be percussed—"In Java fifteen people all with one percussor in their hand and a gong or a drum in front of them, each one playing its own sound while listening to the other: a melody creates itself, beginning of culture."—Polke: "We should learn

from animal behavior—the bowerbird builds its nest with sticks, tall sort of building with an entrance...it's very normal for us to build a house, a nest for the eggs...but the bowerbird builds this nest and at the entrance of it, on the two sides, he collects anything he can find: feathers, cockroach's wings, shiny colored stones...is it a hormonal need in order to mate? Where do the eggs go? Is there any room at all for the eggs in this building? All we know is that they have very specialized collections of brightly colored shiny things of different natures and that they try to push the female through the entrance. Some others have a nest built out of a pile of sticks like a totem, like aborigines, with a totem, in front of which they sit. Other birds have to build a hanging nest...the female might say when it's finished, 'It's no good, start all over again'...I mean it's a big effort for a small bird! Penguins have to bring a good stone to their female...not too easy on the South Pole...." ART—One hundred artists make one artist, says Sigmar: and maybe all this art is for nothing anyway. SIGMAR'S MACHINE FOR PAINTING. All the bottles he has drunk, all the pencils and the rubbish he has used. When he leaves, he tells it to make sure to finish the paintings, but it only keeps on taking up space. MIRRORS. Sigmar likes the idea of the mirror, the mirror of Alice in Wonderland, the mirror of everydayness. He started painting with silver nitrate, one of the chemicals that slowly transforms itself; and wanted to make a mirror in which to paint himself and the room, in the classical Renaissance tradition of Dürer, Van Eyck...(of course you have to choose the angle). He ended up painting these paintings that are absolutely clear. Through the course of time and the transformation of the silver nitrate in contact with the elements, the brush strokes appear. MIRRORS ONCE REMOVED. These new paintings on gauze, transparent gauze painted on both sides, that meet in the middle. SYMMETRIES; OPEN SYMMETRIES. Sigmar collects slices of stones colored and semi-transparent that have rings like trees, compressed; sometimes the core is hollow, sometimes it has a spider web like shattered crystal. They look like photographs of marble walls taken on his trips to the baroque church in Ravenna; or his other photographs of

nature; of trees and grass mirrored in rivers. TRAVELLING—Things to do with perception, in the tradition of the universal man interested in the hidden mechanism of things, in the workings of Nature: human, animal, mineral—

PAPUA SHIELDS

These are shields from specific families. This one here might have the crocodile as a totem; look, it has four legs, but it also looks like a man or a tree or a plant. It's positive and negative, you can see both figures. *Do they have some magic power in battle, are they used in that way?* No, they are used in the house; I think they are sacred. It's like one's name. *So they are like a coat of arms. Are they sacred so that the enemy can't get at you, at your name?* Yes, that's why they use the more inner forms. Look at this: is it a plant? Is it a man? Is it a deer?...Some are more abstract, some more human. They just stand in the house. *Did you get some?* They were sold out!...(laughs) Yes, I have some from Borneo; it's the same thing...look at this, it's a bird, but it's also a man, the man's arm in the bird's neck. *The feet are like plants or like Medusa and the hair is like scorpions. I notice that you have a lot of masks and musical instruments.* I'm looking more for musical instruments because they are not only to look at, they also make sounds. At the exhibition I thought that I would have an instrument in every room; the big gong, the animal, some xylophones I made by myself...different instruments in every room and people can play. It's not forbidden. In one room...blip...blip...in another... boom...boom...together. But it's a question of transport...(laughs)

GLASS WITH URANIUM

What are those glass pieces, mostly yellow and green, that are almost phosphorescent? It's called Canary Glass, it has uranium in it. It used to be quite common until the beginning of the century when it was forbidden. It is very strong, luminous. You can see it from far away. You see this ultraviolet light? You put it on...and you can see them from very far. I bought them in the flea markets. They come from all over; the rabbit comes from Athens...some are from France...this is from Italy...

PLANTS

What is this sort of cooked resin in this pot? It's Kraplag, and was the plant that gave the dye for the trousers that the French army used in the 19th century. I thought if we have a small piece of land we could grow it again! (laughs) But first we tried to identify the plant. We tried, but we weren't sure, because it was a wild plant. The domestic variety doesn't exist anymore. In the 19th century there was a fight between the Dutch and the Polish and the French about this plant...if you look for the industrial farms of these times you see it was the economic basis of these regions...they couldn't make wheat or crops or things, so they made plants you can't eat, because the soil is not fertile. It was a real industry at the time; cities like Toulouse became rich from it. They even had a bronze sculpture of a man standing on the market square with this plant in his hands...I thought there would be some traces of these cultivations...but it's been totally finished for maybe a hundred years. I tried making several different essences...I don't know how it works...I found some wild ones. I crushed them down to obtain the pigment. There is a sketchbook made with this pigment; I also cooked some with rock crystal to densify it; I will use it some other way. *What are these seeds?* They are some Peyote seeds. It is the first one I had that has been flowering for three weeks. *And what is this?* It's peat...it smells very good, but it is not to eat; it is for heating and cooking...it is too complicated to dig it out, the ecologists are against it. *It is so light and it looks like hair; is it fossilized?* They're plants. I don't know how old. *You seem to be very interested in plants.* I've always been. That's how I earned my first money when I was six years old. I had been gathering black wheat grains for a while. I had an enormous box full of it. My mother found out

and she was very upset, because they can be a very potent drug. So she took the whole box to the pharmacist and he bought it all. It was more than two kilos. We lived in Eastern Germany and there weren't any pharmaceutical industries. So the medicines were mostly made from plants. *And what are these black grains? I always remember being told not to touch them or put them in my mouth when I was small.* It's a mutation of wheat that comes from a mushroom that grows in wheat fields. The spores sometimes find an ideal ground on grain and cause this mutation. It is called *claviceps purpurae* and is a very powerful hallucinogenic. It is used for a lot of drugs.

CHEMICALS

And what is the purple dust that you have all over the studio? Britta was telling me that when there is a mouse in the studio you can see purple traces all over. It's a normal pigment; you have it in some pencils. It's the same pigment that you find in those markings on meat. *What is it called?* Diasoxine; it's a color that comes from bitumen. *It's extracted from bitumen and it's purple!* It's violet but ambivalent. I don't know how it works, but the structure can change. It's gold-green sometimes; it has a micro-process behavior, like opal: if you look from one side it's green and if you look from the other side it's red; it's a special structure reflecting the light with a special triangle. You can get it all with a pencil...if you mark very softly, the line is violet...if you make it a little bit stronger it becomes green... with the brush you can make the color yellow metallic gold. *And so the mouse was co-existing with this purple and you could see each of his movements from the tracks.* There was a loaf of bread that I had on my table and they made a hole into it and disappeared inside. The hole

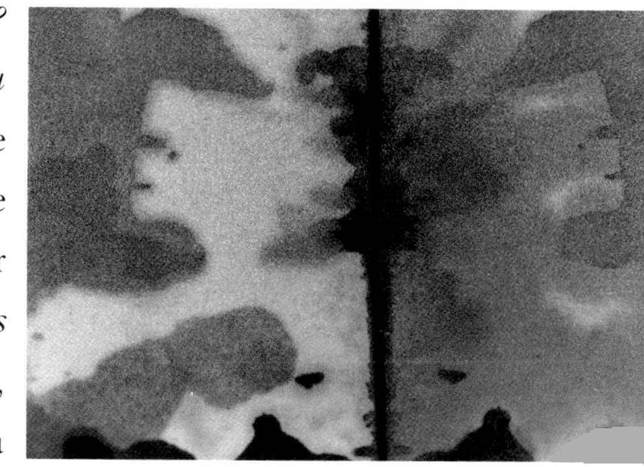

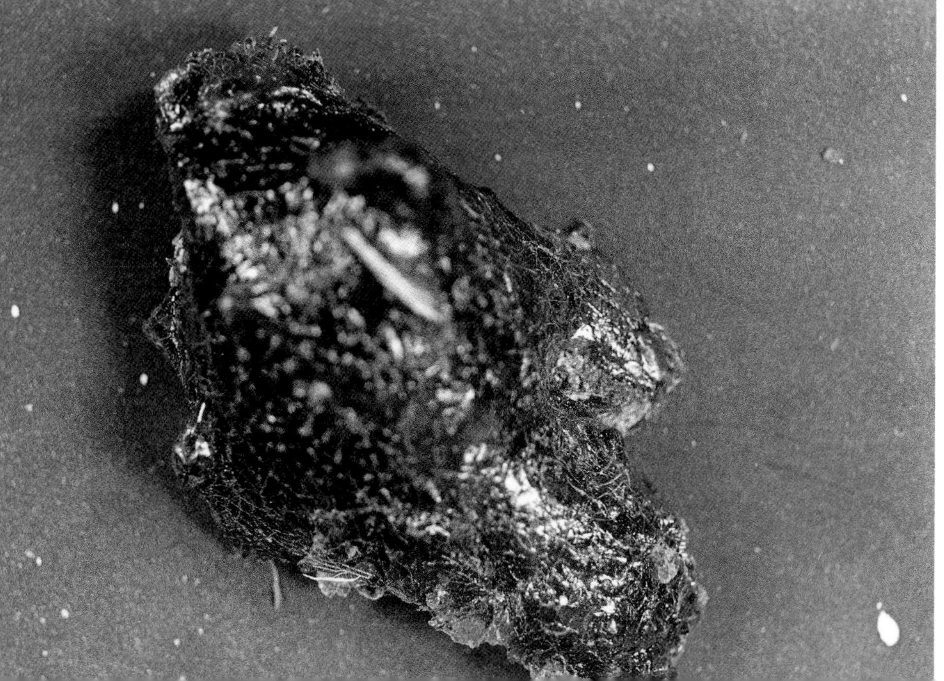

in the bread was small, but it was completely colored from the pigment...I waited; they came out, and they were violet (laughs...both laugh). The fur is like a brush. *Is it the same mouse that makes its nest in your newspaper cuttings?* At this time I have many mice... (laughs)...(laughs again) *What is it that you keep in that lead box?* It is radium. I brought it back myself from Australia and it is very radioactive. *So you keep it in that lead box the whole time?* Yes, it's very strong. I didn't know what to do with it...I learned the old problematic about material...it is not legal...it is not clean...I had no idea what to make, and then from this one I made photos. I had a work from this in the catalogue to Rudy Fuchs' *Documenta*. You put photo paper in it and after three days you have a drawing. You have documented the activity of this mineral. *So it is radioactivity that makes an impression on this paper, without light?* Yes, without light. Just radium. Already in the golden times of Madame Curie they explored these things and came to know what it is. They took photographs with photo paper too; they had sketches and profiles of knives and laboratory instruments. It is very strong...the Geiger counter would go voom... *Do you have a Geiger counter?* Oh yes, I do. I use it a lot.

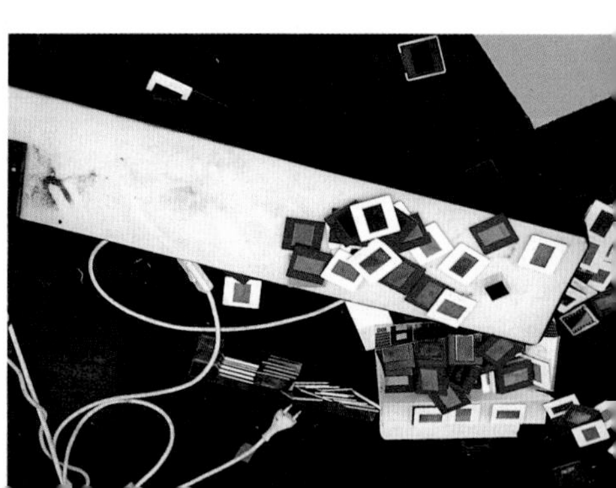

LOCKING UP FULL ROOMS

You work a lot with photographs, take them, juxtapose them, paint them; and I heard you have taken videos of your friends for many years. On your travels, you also take photographs and juxtapose them and make films with it. You must have a lot of material stored away. Do you have a special room for all that, and a darkroom? No, I pile everything up, all the accumulated material...all the things from my travel...and then when the room is filled I lock it up and move on to an empty one. My films I keep together, but I have done this all my life. When I was seven the war broke out and the village I lived in was right on the Russian front. We had to leave immediately and left everything behind. I still remember the drawer of my table with all my things in it: pieces of wood I carved, stones, seeds, a stuffed owl...all left. Then I married and again I left everything I had piled up. Full rooms, one locks them up and leaves...it will be catalogued one day.

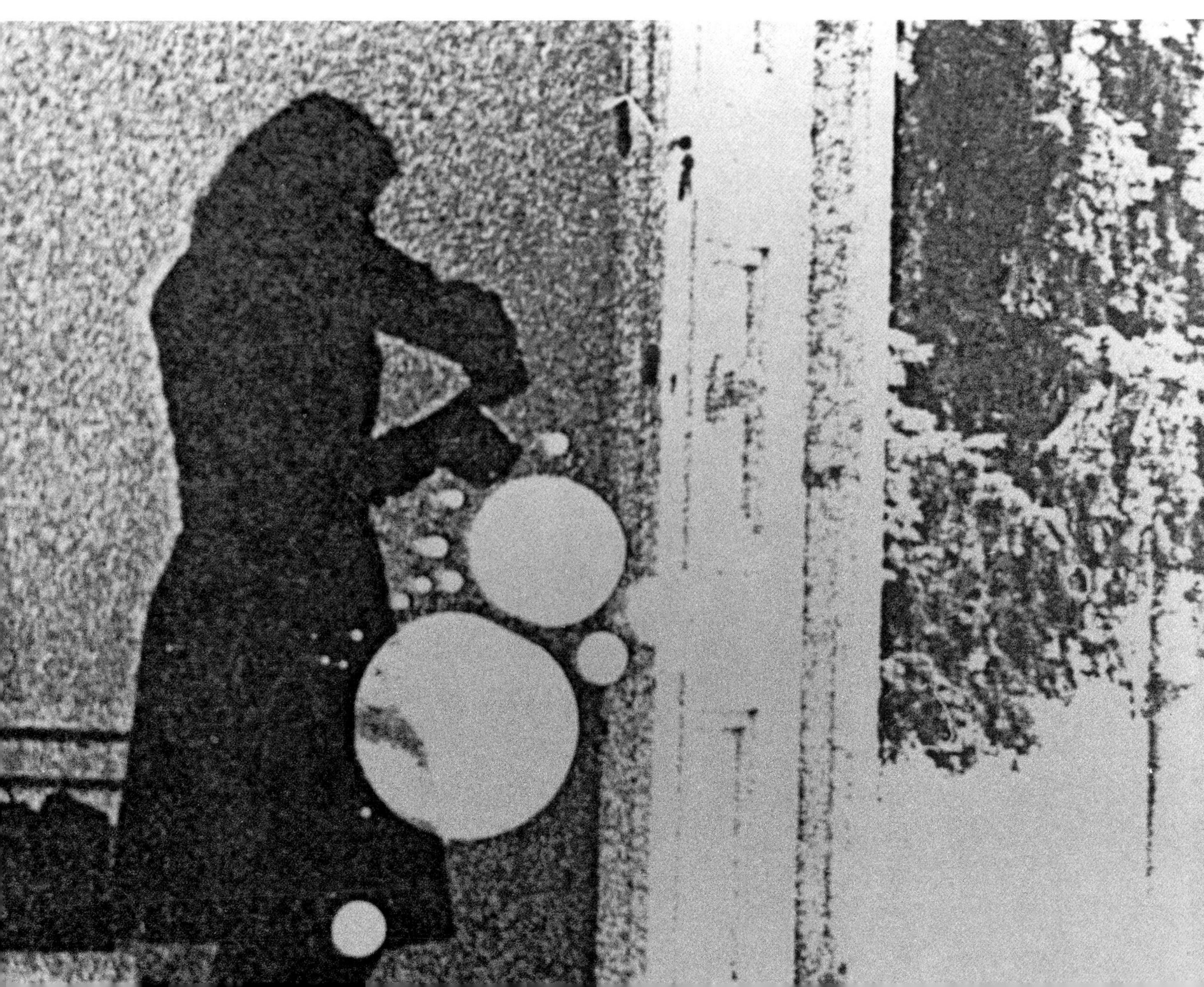

ERRORS

(Looking at the collection of large newspaper errors)...Look at this. It looks like a nougat, and this one looks like an embryo. Their shapes seem to be recurrent and are very peculiar. *How do you explain that?* I have no explanation, because it is new for me too; I'm only collecting. In time we will find the theory. *Sometimes you say the error is only in one copy, sometimes not.* Some are in all...look at this: maybe it comes in the category "forms"...special forms. But I have also teleposed errors because the machine, the techno-machine, also makes mistakes, not just the printer. Look at this. This is not a print mistake, it's a repro-mistake...(laughs) *And so you try to separate them into category mistakes?* Yeah, yeah. There are some categories...often the mistake can be declared depending on the motive, but with others I have no ideas. Look at this Buddha's tooth...I think it's from Tapiez. When the mistakes are very small, I take the photo and blow them up. Then I can see more clearly...it's from separate motives.

PAINTINGS

(Going through his paintings just piled up on his walls)...This is painted with the material that turns from blue to pink. *Oh, like those little figures of dogs that you put out on the balcony to see what the weather is going to be?* Exactly, it's the same thing. I painted this wall and sometimes it's red and sometimes it's blue...the air is very humid here and it works...in the morning it's red and during the day, when the air becomes normal, it gets blue...it's not so quick but after some hours you can see it. *What is the name of that material?* Cobalt chlorine. *In this painting is it here that the color changes?* Yes, it's there; but it's not pure...(taking out another painting)...This is painted with silver oxide...wait, I have another one, I think it works better. This is also not pure, but it is the right color...(taking out another painting)...These are all mixtures I made; this is a studio. For me, in this kind of painting, it is not the color that is important...it is the cracquelé I made...and if you make this it's only grey.

HUMAN SCHICKSAL

Here's a collection of letters. I bought them from a man in Poland. They were written during the war between Poland and Russia. *Were they all written by one man? And who was he writing to?* A Frau Helena Weldelz...his wife?...he didn't come back. 1940 to 1942: three years...he wasn't allowed to say where they were, not allowed to write about war matters. It's all impersonal, but sometimes you can understand what they meant and what they thought. They're really documents about Poland. *And this is the box they were in?* Yeah, human Schicksal. *What is Schicksal?* The human way of life; the way of life of one soldier...that's what is left... material...it may be essential.

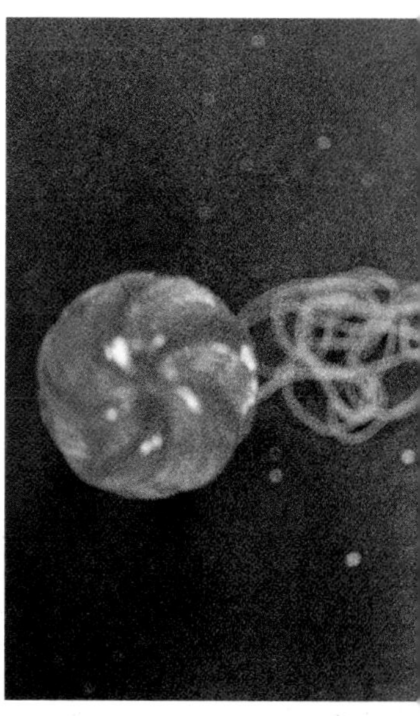

CROWS
FIYING
THE BLACK
FLAG OF
THEM
SELVES

Julian Schnabel

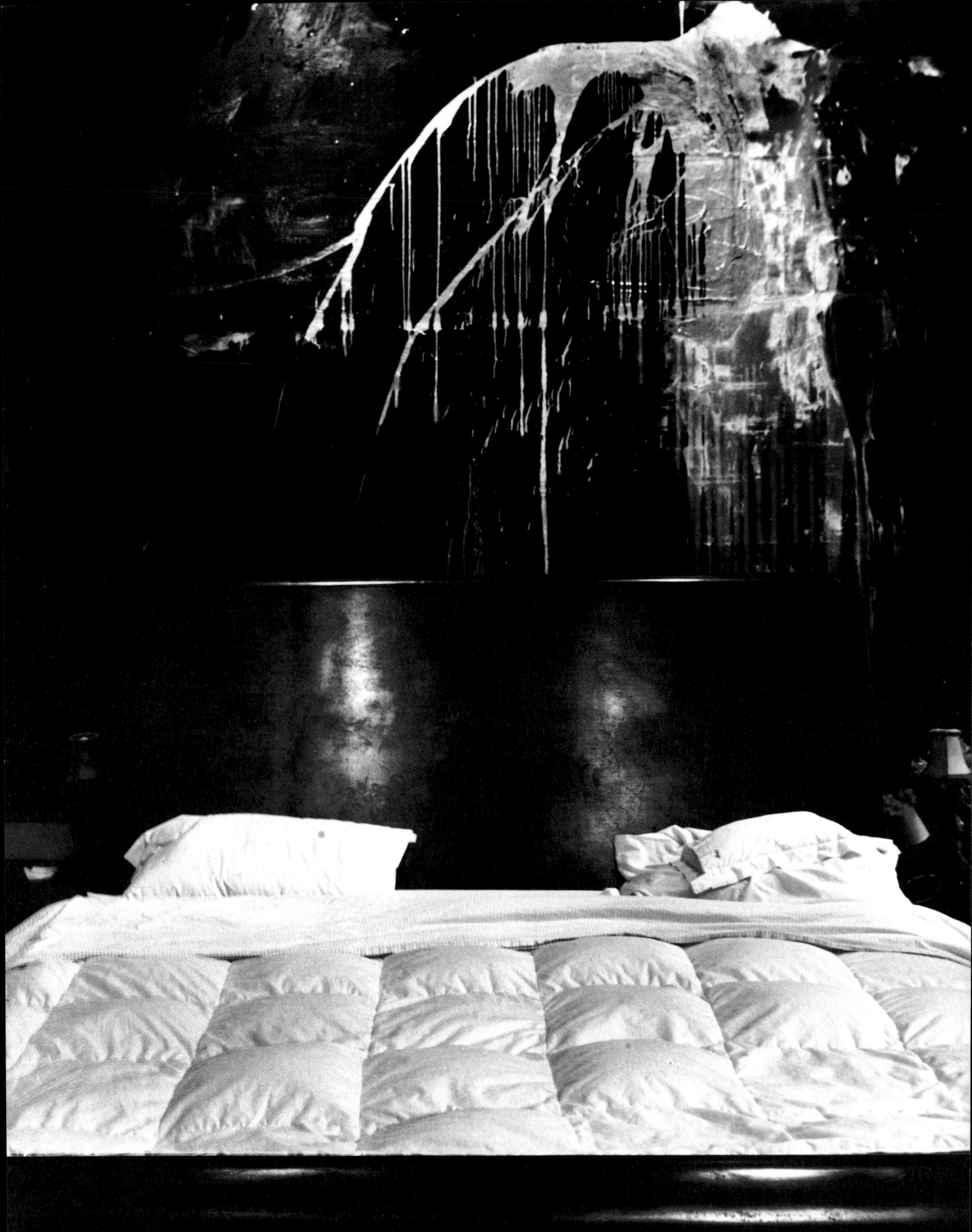

A

STRAW DOGS
LA BALANCE
BELLISIMA
LITTLE BIG MAN

TURBA

FLA
UN
JU
VJ

Valerio
JS-R85

Paola: You have what looks like a ruin in front of your house. How did it come about? Julian: I wanted to build some place that looked like it was already there—some place I had been to that I liked. I immediately saw it when we first came here, and I felt it would remind me of somewhere I wanted to be. There was a Green and Green house....They were these two brother architects who made things in California in the first part of the century. They were inspired by walls, by Hadrian's villa, for example. They made different gardens for people, gardens with stone and brick that felt like places in Italy. The ruin here is like different places I have been to, or I wanted to make it like some place where I thought I'd been but I hadn't...an accumulation of feelings about different places. Sometimes it looks like it's in Italy, sometimes Mexico. It depends on the quality of the light that day. It also looks like it could be a stone house in New York State that belonged to my grandmother, but she never had a house in upstate New York. I just wanted to build some kind of a dream-like place that I wished I remembered but don't. It was like building fiction; a place that had been in my family for generations, and that I used to go to when I was young, but since I didn't have that, I had to make it up. Someone told me they couldn't believe that a place like this could exist without having been here for generations, and that has to do with a sediment of feeling, a sediment of history, the way objects look in particular places, a compression of feelings and memory. There are so many different things to look at or to build or to focus on, and you have to select where you want to be, what you want to look at. Some people want to make money, some people want to be the fastest swimmer in the world, some people want to be left alone, some people want to make things so that they can disappear...while making them. It is a form of escapism, you know—it is and it isn't. Look at this painting. (showing a photograph). It looks very much like that wall. It's a sort of continuation. I physically put each stone in that wall, with Giuseppe the gardener and his son John. I did it intuitively. I used the bricks as a way of isolating the shape of different stones, to make the stones into a drawing. I selected the materials; I had a sort of image in my head. I stopped when it looked right. *You have said about time: "The materiality of a work of art is just part of a desire, only important as a quality of being, a feeling, a meaning, a recognition, which is described by and describes the time it had been made in, something human." You have also spoken about similarities of feelings in different works, early Beuys with early Twombly, for example.* Similarities of need, similarities of

appearance...look (shows a drawing). 1975...looks like a plaster wall near a ship channel in Galveston. *Yes, and you have said: "Over and over these similarities make up the human stream of things, which constitutes the history of objects."* That sounds pretty good! But look. (showing a painting) It looks like it could be here. It's actually red and white and plaster. Don't you think it looks Italian? And that was made before I went to Italy! *All the cracked walls...* It's funny. Look. This too. (showing another drawing) Before I ever went. It's just something that you feel, some sort of memory and desire. I'm very uncomfortable in a lot of places. So I guess I needed to make a place very insulated, internal. I had to make it peaceful, something I can forget myself in, something where everything is right, every placement, the agreement between a vase sitting somewhere and the stones, how they fit on the grass. I need a satisfying organization of things so I don't have to think about them, so I can escape, particularly because I think the world outside is so horrifying. At the same time, the things made in this place must clarify certain truths, justify their existence out in the world. I think most people do that, or artists do that: they build someplace, like a think tank or something, where they can haunt their own houses, become their own ghosts, a particular place where they can be, where there is no stoppage, no things that stop the flow of the impulse. *In the things you build and in your work in general you borrow from many different sources. Things look familiar and yet they make one feel displaced. There is great freedom in this, and mystery too; your mystery, that speaks of other mysteries.* I'm looking for something, and you have to unearth the things you are looking for—something strange and unfamiliar and something familiar. How can it seduce you if it's completely foreign? And yet it has to be something that is unlike you to make you realize yourself. Someone was saying, "Why does he paint on other things, why doesn't he paint on canvas?" Everybody who makes paintings is looking for some kind of image that one hasn't seen. If I think that I can get further out through using other materials, why not? Why should we have any sort of rules that would keep us from finding what we have no idea about anyway? I'm looking for something that's further. I have already done all

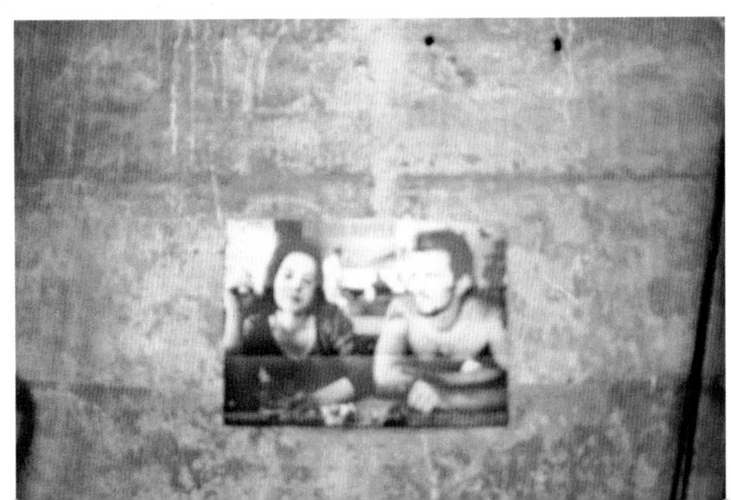

the work, and now I just need to do some more. I am literally doing the opposite of what all the American painters are doing: They are all trying to find this image that identifies them as *them*. I'm looking for the image that I want to find in everybody else...as part of everything else. When I was in India, for example, I found this tanka in Nepal, and I had an Indian photographer come to my hotel room and take pictures of details from it. I asked some Indian sign painters to paint details of these images. When I gave them the full picture instead of the detail, they painted a clichéd idea of it, but if I gave them a picture that was incomplete, then they couldn't see the outline of it, so they couldn't make it as a clichéd version. Because they had never looked at just one part of it before, they had to use their best technique to paint this peculiar thing I asked them to paint, and the weird way it configurated was exactly what I was interested in. Then I see these things as drawings for other paintings. Look at that big foot there, for example; it's one of the Indian sign paintings. Look how the lines are painted on the left hand side. That's exactly what I'm looking for in my paintings.

How do you select your objects? They just come to me. I don't even look for them. People bring them to me. It seems they've got more of an idea of what I'm doing than I do! For example, I made a painting on a carnival banner some while ago. Akira Ikeda saw it, and when he saw the backdrops of the Kabuki Theater he thought about the painting, so they sent me pictures of this material and asked me if I wanted it. I guess you put an idea in the world and somebody sees something somewhere and then they think that it has to do with you, so they give you back something. Like these tarps with tape on them—they are from the Gramercy Park Gym. James Nares saw my Mexican paintings on this material and, when he was in the gym, and they were throwing these out, he thought, "I guess Julian could make paintings with them." So he brought them over. I was driving down the street in Mexico, and there was a truck broken down, and I saw a tarp lying right in front of me, so I stopped the car and bought it from the truck driver. I just run into these objects. One thing I like about these tarps is that there is a great depth of field. They look like there's a desert in them. I think photographers often used backdrops to create a sense of space in photographs, like Irving Penn, for example. I like the fact that they look like things already, that the world has affected them. I like old things; I like the way they're made. It is hard to find new things that I like. Maybe something is wrong with me. Even

the new things I make look like they're old. Old things make me feel more classical, more comfortable; they make me feel outside of time. It removes me from noise. On the other side, I think that these other paintings with the writing on them look very much like signs in Nicaragua or San Salvador, some kind of banner. They have this political look to them. As paintings they seem very extreme: you can't tell if they're paintings or not paintings.

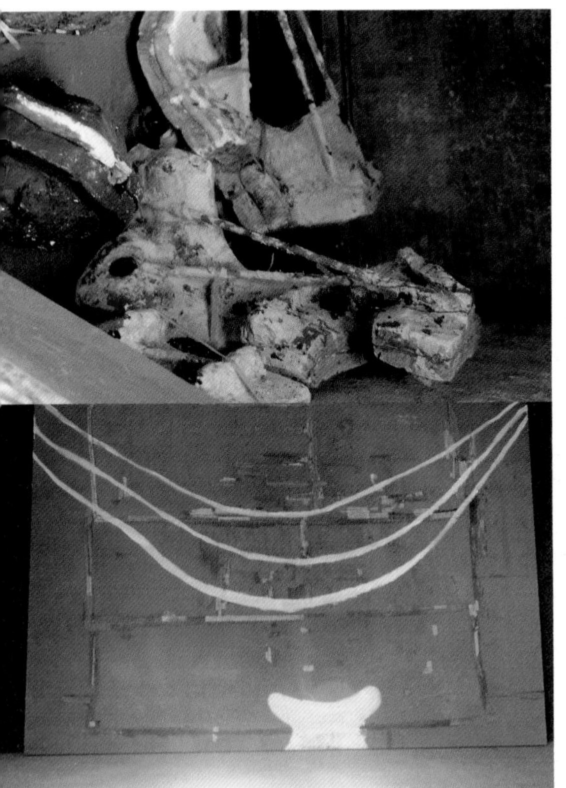

They also have a feeling of having been left outside, left over. *So much openness to the internal life of things and yet so balanced...* I like to have complete control over what the things I make look like, but I don't want them to look composed. I want them to comfort me or show me something that's outside of myself. I want a clarity in the fabric of the fiction that exists. I don't want it to show where I've done something and of course it does show where I did it, but somehow I have a communion with the materials and with the kind of drawings that exist in it and I really get immersed in it, lost in it. I guess it's anthropological art, anthropomorphic art. They just have that quality of humanness and, to get back to your question, I guess that's what I select. I can't really put my finger on it; there are different shapes that I think are formed by some kind of pressure of gravity. There are a million different permutations of human behavior and objects that are the residue of these different kinds of behavior, and I guess I'm selecting things that are charged in some way or affected in some way. I paint like an Indian sign painter. I imagine what the boss might tell the guy to paint, what jobs he could give them to do, so that I can make paintings that come from another place...then I can enter into that...then I can travel. *Like in the house...* Yes, like in the house—the same feeling of wanting to be somewhere else, somebody else's place...wanting to be in another painting...not your painting. I build this house and make these paintings, but the reason we're building these things is because we're disappearing, and we want to witness ourselves disappearing, and we want to feel the right way while disappearing. This residue, these feelings about human activities, seem to be the only thing we have if we don't believe in heaven. And we can only try to go further through the materiality of the work, through a quality of tenuousness, to arrive at something like a vision to improve the quality of seeing the world. With that realization, you think that you made the right choice. I mean, you could be anything you want as long as you don't become invisible and start flying around the room.

Wolfgang Laib

The greatest revelation has to come out of your own daily life. There it has to begin and there it has to be achieved—and then it will not end...

WOLFGANG LAIB

स्व. ब्रह्मचारी जीवराज गौतमचंदजी दोशी
संस्थापक, जैन संस्कृति संरक्षक संघ, शोलापूर

Paola: Pollen is at the center of much of your work. Since it's found seasonally and takes a long time to gather, has it given your life and work special rhythms? Wolfgang: I collect the pollen in early spring; sometimes even in early January when the hazel-nut trees begin to blossom. I collect it through the spring and early summer up to mid-June or the end of June, nearly every day if it's not raining. Then in late summer and fall I'm working with my stones. I grind down the milkstones by hand, outside near the pond, and I work with other things like the beeswax pieces, and think of the things I'm interested in making. Then in winter the days are very quiet and I like to stay here or travel or have exhibitions. *Collecting pollen must be different from day to day.* Very different. There are days when there is a lot of pollen and there are days that have very little pollen. It depends on the wind and the sun. *You were saying that last year the weather was so warm you were able to gather in one week what it normally would have taken you three weeks to gather, but what if there's wind for a few weeks? You could lose the whole season.* That's not the point—losing or winning—it's something different. It's not about collecting as much as possible. My work is very different for the concept of work in our culture. Sometimes I collect a lot and that's beautiful; sometimes I get very little and that's beautiful too. *Life-essence has a lot to do with you and your work, with your family and the way you live. How did your opening towards it start?* First I studied medicine and then I became very disappointed with it. My concerns or the things I find really important have never changed. What I was searching for in medicine was the same thing that I am searching for now, but because I changed, I couldn't believe anymore in a science that took the body only in such a material way, where the hand, for example, is only a material thing. My work...what I did then, was what I believe about my life, about my body; so when I use milk or pollen, I'm really rejecting what happened in twentieth-century medicine. *You lived in India for a number of years when your father was working on a program for finding water in Indian villages. Was being in India when your were young important for you?* My father sponsored a program for rural development and our family had to live in a close relationship to this context, which is very difficult for Europeans. It was an important time for us, for the whole family, and it changed us. But then, of course, our relationship to India was always very open. Lots of things which for other people seem very Indian in my work, or very Asian, are really...it's very complex somehow, because these things which you can find now in India were found in Italy and Germany in the thirteenth century, but not now. They are

things which I really love and which we can still find now elsewhere. When I see Australian aborigines, these things are all there. The things that can change our lives are very far from our actual society, and so I'm much more interested in things that have nothing to do with our society. I think they have a lot of power to make something completely different for our future, for our real life. Not that I am fleeing the responsibilities of actual life; but the more it can be different from what it is now, the more impact it can have on making a real change. I believe in a real change; I think it's time, not just to continue on in one way, with all these concepts...all these things are really centuries old and there's nothing new happening. There is much happening, and a lot of very

important things too, but at the level where there is no possibility of a real change in all these concepts: how we see what things are, what they are not. *The flow of life, as we experience it these days, is so fractured. Yet, in your family it feels so full and there is so much communication without words. It's something you find more of in some cultures than in others.* Yes, I think you don't find that in our culture right now. I can't say I really find something wrong in this culture, but I find many things very wrong...I see that four centuries after the Renaissance our culture is still continuing with it. At its time, of course, the Renaissance was something incredible, powerful and very, very beautiful. But then it continued and it has been putting detail over detail, and no real change has happened since. I think that after four or five hundred years there is the possibility of a real new beginning, as the Renaissance was. It's very exciting and beautiful to hope and work for something that could bring about a totally different ideal of what you are and what you do and how you feel. When I collect pollen, for example, I'm not creating pollen, I'm just collecting it, putting it out. So I'm part of this whole and I'm not claiming I'm the creator of these things. This, of course, was very powerful in our culture, this concept of the individual who is responsible and who does what he has, but has not what he does not. It's also a tragedy, a very tragic end when you are only an individual and nothing else. You're

disconnected from everything. All the other cultures didn't have this. They really had a connection to everything and the individual was within everything. I think that is extremely beautiful. We need a different idea of time and of what to do in time, of what you want to accomplish and progress in; all these things are just turned around here. It's not a question of accomplishing something in so much time, or of having this after that in this or that time. It is, I think, quite the opposite, and you're totally free of all these things. It's quite a challenge. Time, for these plants, or for me, or the time I work out there collecting pollen, is all very relative after all; it's the opposite of the concepts we now have about these things. It's not a thesis, it's not that I have a certain philosophy or ideology. It just comes out of...of pollen, of milk. So if you really take these things, take them as they are, you become similar to, say, what a plant is. A tree stands there, a forest, and they don't move...it's a matter of becoming similar to something like that. Already there is so much change in you, but towards something so totally different, also being open to so much. For me art is not something on the wall; that is very rare. The point of it is when it really changes your daily life, what you do and what your life is. With the milkstone, for example, filling a milkstone or grinding it. if you really love it, when you actually do it you come closer and more like such a milkstone yourself. I'm not doing these things for myself. I really want to show it to somebody else and include other people, that it's possible for others to fill a milkstone, sift some pollen; that you become part of it, part of the surface of the pollen, part of the surface of the milk. Otherwise, it seems so remote, so different, so far away from people's lives. But it's such a beautiful challenge to move towards...being not just at the service of yourself. *You have a beautiful vegetable garden and many flowers. One has to really care for them, be there and watch them grow. Is this what you like about gardens and growing things?* Yes, of course. It's the opposite of what artists thought thirty years ago, being free of all these things. But if you are, then it's time to change completely and care for something and have an incredible attention to something or a relationship. *This house you live in; it feels like the outside is inside, as if there were no walls, just glass, and nature all around. How was it built?* It was built by my parents when I was ten years old. They wanted to have a home,

but then it became what it is, quite different from a normal home. It was designed by a Swiss architect. It has something very special, this connection to the outside, to the land around, the living inside so close to the life outside; it's in the combination of form and shape and the living in it, together with the land and plants and all the vegetation around. *When did you start gathering pollen?* That was in 1977. In 1974 I left the medical school and some months later I made my first milkstone, and then three years later I started gathering pollen. *Did you have a studio where you worked?* No, I had no place to have a studio. But back then I really loved not being fixed in a special space. I really loved being free and outside all the time. But in the course of time I found I had things I didn't know where to put, and then the opportunity to have a space came along. But to me a studio is more a space where I can be a certain time with some of my things, sometimes working...but the studio is mostly empty...it's just to be by myself, alone with some of my pieces: one pollen piece, one milkstone. *What are these small brick-like pieces?* Those come directly from the bee-keepers. They leave the honeycomb in the sun and the beeswax slowly melts down into whatever shape, sometimes very beautiful, simple shapes. The first pieces I made I bought these shapes from the bee-keeper and just melted them together. The first larger pieces I made were houses with very thin metal on the outside and wood on the inside, and rice inside. They refer somehow to the reliquaries of the Middle Ages, but then instead of the bones of the saints I had the real food, which is somehow really very different. Later I made these houses out of sealing wax usually used for letters, with extremely intense colors and the rice totally sealed off. The food is sealed off from your own body; your body outside, and the food inside the house. *And the black stones you showed me in the other room...* That's from the first pieces I made with rice and it's called "Sixty-three Rice Meals For A Stone." It was composed of sixty-three plates with mountains of rice, one mountain of pollen, and the stones. Real meals for the stones. Meals are not only for the body; food is something much more open: stones also need food. Things are connected differently than we think. The "Sixty-three" refers to the sixty-three saints in South Indian mythology. They were mostly ascetics whose lives were more concerned with fasting than with eating, and more about another kind of body than this one. My most recent piece is a beeswax space called "For Another Body," which relates to such things. Food is something essential for the body, it somehow maintains the body, but of course we can't really define this energy. I think the body is

only a receptacle for something else. In Christianity we see Christ coming out of the tomb with his hands crossed, standing above the tomb with his body. That's exactly where Europeans, Christians, started getting beyond the human body, going beyond death, not only as a metaphor, but beyond the body itself. What I find so beautiful are those crossed arms, as if everything were done and there was nothing more to do. You find it in the Italian paintings of the thirteenth and fourteenth centuries. *And "For Another Body," this large space you are building now, where a whole person can go inside a beeswax house...* The title means of course that you experience your body inside, but with the hope that this body is not the final stage of yourself...the wish for another body for yourself, that you are not this body alone, that there is something else. Of course for me it's also beautiful to see such things so clearly shown and lived with Christians six hundred years ago. The proportion of the space is like a tomb, very narrow and very high, with the intense color of the beeswax. So narrow, but you have this mystical height that takes you away again. *It reminds me more of the Muslim tomb of the mystic poet Rumi. When did your interest in Rumi and Konia first begin?* I was eighteen or nineteen. The situation there is very strange. In 1925 I think the Sufi order was prohibited by law. From then on the main mosque and the main place where this order was founded was turned into a museum where you had to pay an entrance fee. Even today thousands of people come to that mosque in Konia and pay the fee. But for them it's like a pilgrimage, and they kiss the tomb of Rumi, and they just don't care. And the Turkish government tries to make the dance of the whirling dervishes into a performance for tourists. They weren't allowed to dance in the mosque, they had to dance in a football stadium. *Are there other places that have touched you?* Yes, another one is the center of Jain worship in India. It is a religion like Buddhism which has had a very real influence on me for a long time. There I was, studying medicine, having this extreme connection, this touch with flesh, and during the weekends I would read the scriptures of the Jains. I was deeply touched by their extreme non-violence and the extreme purity they speak about and which their nuns and monks live very deeply. It was such an extreme opposite of what I was doing, that I couldn't believe anymore in medicine and the taking of flesh, how it's done in science. Western art historians haven't written much about Jain art because for them it's mostly uninteresting, nearly boring. A Jain artist has a totally different idea of what's important in making a statue. The artist portrays a Jain saint, how are they called, *titankara*...if a *titankara* has one face, the next *titankara* has the same face. There's no difference; so it's not a

different portrait, it's just that if a *titankara* has achieved a certain inner mind, it shows on the outside with a face, but the next saint has the same face. There's no difference. It's as if the saints had achieved a certain inner mind that shows on the outside, and so one statue is exactly the same as the other. Now that's something extremely beautiful, but in our culture it seems entirely boring. *Did you grow up as a vegetarian?* No, that came with studying medicine. It was this contact with flesh and with dead bodies that made me over the years so sensitive to all these things. Therefore, studying medicine was really very important for me, much more important than going to art college or something like that. It changed my whole idea of the body, of material things and life. Half a year after I left medical school I did my first milkstone. It was a direct answer and response to what I had seen. It was like an instant cleaning-out. A half a year before I had worked on a dissertation on medical hygiene and the purity of drinking water in South India, and then half a year later I understood what purity was. For me a stone is a living being, like a plant, or like a human being or an animal. I don't really see that much difference. I admire a plant as much as a human, as a living being, just like the stones too. It's not my idea; a thousand years ago you could find the same idea, and it's still in Australia, people seeing in a rock living beings or their ancestors. It's not the point to invent new philosophies. I think it's just there; you just have to see it. *Are there any other places you visit?* Last year I went to Assisi in Italy to the tomb of St. Francis. It

had an enormous impact on me, and finally, a few months ago, I began the recent piece lined with beeswax that you can enter. What struck me was the chapel St. Francis had fixed up outside Assisi being surrounded by this big baroque church. Also the very small spaces left over from the time of St. Francis. It's beautiful for me to see the size and proportion of these very small but intense spaces, only two, three, four meters at the most, but incredibly full. And then you have a huge baroque church just totally empty. You see the power of the Popes...but I think you see the difference. *I see you read from a lot of very different sources. What are the things that interest you most?* Different things, like Rumi, or St. Francis or Australian aboriginal things...mostly I'm interested in what gives me the feeling that it's far from our own situation. Not fleeing contemporary life, but having that and a future life that contains something very different for our life, especially our life in the future. I'm not interested in what seems to be the problems of the moment, or the interesting things discussed every day in the newspaper. That I find boring. For politicians there are actual problems, things have to be solved. But what's the next step...finally I think that's why I became an artist. I think art really has this incredible openness. I still hope, sometimes I'm very disappointed, but I still hope that in art you can have this wishing for something else, but something that comes into reality for your own life. *I haven't seen you listening to much music...do you?* I like dervish music and listen to it a lot, and some Indian music too. I don't care for Western classical music, going to an opera, for example, as much as I like the human voice...but reciting inside a theater...it's the opposite of the photograph I showed you of the Indian boy rehearsing his music in the mountains, playing for the stones.

Captions For Full-Page Photos

Louise Bourgeois Louise's portrait with darned cuffs by Paola Igliori...Mantlepiece...Spools sculpture...Styrofoam sculpture sitting on radiator...Shopping cart with sculptures and various things...A tree as a portrait of a friend...Marble breasts and cutting instruments...The Linen Room...Louise's writings to herself...Portrait in Louise's bedroom...Child's body with bullet holes, hemp...Sculptures in Louise's studio...Portrait of her husband inside velvet involucre...Dismembered parts of the body (mannequin hanging between closets)...Ladders...Stones from the river as basement floor...Junction box—Things that make the house function...Louise's Studio (door made by Louise)...Collection of everyday utensils—meatgrinders used as woodclamps...The Shewolf (portrait of her mother)...Flowers and Stairs...Cutting instruments (drawing by Louise)...Writing to herself that Louise always kept on her desk.

James Turrell Turrell's portrait (he is a Quaker)...People in spacesuits...Entrance door to Turrell's Skystone Foundation...Inside Roden Crater...A Room in the cabin where Turrell lives in Flagstaff, Arizona...Turrell's room with flying utensils and controls...Ready to go—oxygen, space suit, various instruments and aerial cameras...Goya's etching from one of Turrell's books...More instruments...Book from Turrell's library...Sky from one of Turrell's installations...Truck part that he's restoring...Grinding tips and other tools...Varnish...Altitude readings...Childhood treasures and others...The house where the family lives...Glider...Topographical model...Cloud formations...Roden Crater from a distance...Trucks and Cars restored by Turrell...Nightfall on the edge of the crater.

Enzo Cucchi Portrait with shadow—like clouds over land...Enlargement of view outside the studio... Bedroom in Ancona.

Vito Acconci Self portrait...Vito's main room...Boat and bicycles...Vito's bed...Vito's fish next to the bed...The sound room—occasional resting place...Various details...Views out of Vito's window... The *Encyclopedia Britannica* as a broomstand...Vito's western magazine-encyclopedia done at age 12...Vito's Library—From Body to Revolution—65 categories...The 65 categories...A pile of stools...Glass piece from Snow White's flower bed..."Overstuffed Chair", 1987...Vito's poetry.

Cy Twombly Portrait taken by his wife in the sixties...Exterior of the house...Entrance hall with Roman sculpture...Detail of Twombly's painting *The Wilder Shores of Love*...Twombly's photograph of the inner garden...Twombly's sculpture...Unfinished paintings in the studio...Colors, lucky rat...The Studio just after...A room in the house (warriors, still and moving)...Head of Dionysus (photo by Twombly)...Painting...Meteoric stone...Twombly's polaroids...Looking at a frame...An Etruscan fragment, etc....Photos by Twombly of rooms in the house and his bedroom...Twombly's sculpture at the foot of his bed...Apollo (drawing)... Carpenter working on window and Roman sculpture...Portico in the courtyard...Pan...Detail of painting...Sequence of rooms...Twombly's sculpture of perked-up tulip...Roman Head...Twombly's drawing...Twombly's sculptures and shutters ajar.

Gilbert & George Portrait...Shoe-vase...Outside of Gilbert and George's House...Gilbert and George's parlor...Vases...Around G & G...Vases and details...More around G & G...Models that G & G built of the Museums where they have shows, in order to plan the installations...*Life, Fear, Hope, Death*...Color test from Annie Besant, *Thought Forms,* published by Theosophical Society.

Francesco Clemente Clemente's reflection in metal Indian suitcase...Studio...His corner delimitated by Frank Lloyd Wright sofa-library...Oceanic sculpture...Shoes, slippers, and fruit...Column and boxes...Mamma and madonna...Images, small poems...Mexican magic powder bags...Details...Bench and bowl..."Purgatory"...Ramana Maharshi comic book.

Sigmar Polke Sigmar...Kopf, 1966...Room being filled...Enlarged landscape (photo by Polke)...Nature mirrored (photo by Polke)...Newspaper cuttings (photo by Polke)...Image from newspaper error collection (photo by Polke)...Big gold nuggets (photos by Polke).

Julian Schnabel An eye-detail of plate painting...Portrait...Fake ruin...Plate paintings in nature...Empty chairs, Long Island...Sculpture and trees, Long Island...Julian...Looking out on New York street...Oceanic masks, fifties fabric...Roman bust, Warhol portrait...Two chairs in front of painting...A room...Bed and velvet splash painting...Children's room...Door handles...Artaud's portrait by Man Ray...Rene Ricard's portrait by Julian...Alan Vega sculpture, etc....Studio..."Valerio" painting, 1985.

Wolfgang Laib Gathering pollen...Life objects...Watering the seeds...A room—inside and outside... The pond...A book...Pollen piece...Beeswax bricks...His studio...Rumi's Tomb..."Sixty-Three Saints" (photo by Laib)...Titankara (photo by Laib)...A milkstone (photo by Laib)...Rehearsing for the stones (photo by Laib).

Louise Bourgeois was born in Paris in 1911. She studied art at the Ecole des Beaux-Arts and numerous ateliers in Paris until her marriage to Robert Goldwater in 1938, when she moved to New York and resumed her studies at the Art Students League. Bourgeois' first solo exhibition at the Bertha Schaefer Gallery, New York, in 1945 featured twelve paintings. The artist began experimenting with large-scale sculpture in the early 1940s and began exhibiting her distinctive biomorphic sculpture in 1953 at Peridot Gallery. Since that time Bourgeois has been the subject of numerous solo shows at galleries including Xavier Fourcade and most recently at the Robert Miller Gallery and Galerie Lelong. She has also been included in countless group exhibitions, including the Whitney Museum of American Art Annual from the years 1953 to 1957 and its "200 Years of American Sculpture" exhibition in 1976, in which her sculpture played a substantial part. Bourgeois has been the subject of two major retrospectives in the last decade; one organized by the Museum of Modern Art, New York, in 1982 (travelling to the Contemporary Arts Museum, Houston; Museum of Contemporary Art, Chicago; Akron Art Museum, Akron) and another originating at the Frankfurter Kunstverein, Frankfurt, West Germany, in 1989 (travelling to Städtische Galerie im Lenbachhaus, Munich, West Germany; Kunstmuseum, Lucerne, Switzerland; Musée St. Pierre, Lyon, France; Fundación Tàpies, Barcelona, Spain). Louise Bourgeois received an Honorary Doctorate from Yale University in 1977; she has taught art at numerous universities and art schools. She currently lives and works in New York City.

James Turrell was born in Los Angeles, California, in 1943. He graduated from Pomona College in 1965 with a degree in perceptual psychology, and pursued graduate studies in art at the University of California, Irvine, and Claremont Graduate School, receiving a master's degree from the latter in 1973. The artist lived and worked in a studio in Ocean Park, California, between the years 1966 and 1974, where he began to create works of art based on light and space. It was during this period that Turrell first became interested in the mechanics of flying and soaring. During 1968–69, Turrell participated in the art and technology program organized by the Los Angeles County Museum of Art where he worked with fellow California artist, Robert Irwin. He is considered to be one of the initiators of the California Light & Space Movement, a movement in which direct perception is considered a central part of the art experience. Turrell's light and space installations have been exhibited in numerous locations on the East and West Coast and in Europe. The artist has been the subject of a number of major exhibitions, including a one-man show at the Stedelijk Museum, Amsterdam, in 1976, a retrospective at the Whitney Museum of American Art, New York, in

1980, and a retrospective at the Museum of Contemporary Art, Los Angeles, in 1985–86. Other exhibitions include one-man shows at Leo Castelli Gallery, 1981–82; Center on Contemporary Art, Seattle, 1982; Israel Museum, Jerusalem, 1983–83; Kunsthalle, Basel, 1987; and Musée D'Art Contemporain, Nimes, 1989. The artist has been the recipient of several awards including the Guggenheim Fellowship in 1974 and the MacArthur Foundation Fellowship in 1984. Turrell is currently in the process of creating a giant outdoor celestial observatory out of the Roden Crater, a volcanic cinder cone overlooking the edge of the Painted Desert in North Central Arizona. Funding for this project has already been received from the Dia Art Foundation, the Guggenheim Foundation, and the National Endowment for the Arts.

Enzo Cucchi was born in 1950 in the farmland of Italy's Marches region. He still lives and works nearby in the city of Ancona on the shores of the Adriatic Sea. Cucchi, along with Sandro Chia, Francesco Clemente, and Mimmo Paladino, was an important member of the Italian Neo-Expressionist movement which swept New York in 1980. His heavily painted, apocalyptic landscapes were included in "Italian Art Now: An American Perspective," at the Solomon R. Guggenheim Museum in 1982. His work, often incorporating found objects with painted anthropomorphic shapes, is a poetic investigation into the contrast between nature and culture. The artist's work has been included in numerous exhibitions in the United States and abroad. Cucchi was the subject of a major one-man exhibition at the Solomon R. Guggenheim Museum in 1986, as well as solo shows at the Stedelijk Museum, Amsterdam, and Kunsthalle, Basel, in 1983–84; Louisiana Museum of Modern Art, Humlebaek, Denmark, 1985; Centres des Arts Plastiques Contemporaines, Bordeaux, in 1986; Staatsgalerie moderner Kunst, Munich, in 1987; and Marlborough Gallery, New York, in 1989.

Vito Acconci was born in the Bronx, New York, in 1940. He studied classical languages and literature in college and pursued graduate studies at the Writer's Workshop at the University of Iowa. Upon completion of his studies in the mid-1960s he wrote poetry and became co-editor of a literary/art magazine entitled *0 TO 9*. Toward the end of the 1960s his poetry readings were transformed into poetry "events" in which the artist relied heavily on audiotapes and visual props for his presentations. Acconci's early art performances were highly autobiographical, dealing with notions of the self, interpersonal relationships, and his own relationship as an artist to the viewer. By the mid-1970s his work became more sculptural and architectonic, depending on viewer participation to create the proper cultural and interactive context for each site-specific installation. In the last few years the artist has been creating architectural and landscape projects for public areas—streets, municipal buildings, and parks. He has been the focus of several important museum exhibitions including the Kunstmuseum Luzerne, 1978; the Stedelijk Museum, Amsterdam, in 1978; Museum of Contemporary Art, Chicago, in 1980; and the La Jolla Museum of Contemporary Art in 1987. The artist is currently working on a playground in Detroit, a pedestrian mall in Baltimore, and a convention center in St. Louis.

Cy Twombly was born in Lexington, Virginia, in 1928. He studied at Washington & Lee University in Lexington, the Boston Museum School, and the Art Students League in New York City. In 1951 he attended Black Mountain College where he first met poet Charles Olson, and artists Robert Motherwell and Franz Kline (both his teachers), and Robert Rauschenberg with whom he established a lifelong friendship. Twombly then travelled with Rauschenberg throughout Spain, Morocco, and Italy in 1952. It was at that time that he first immersed himself in the classical wonders and sensual pleasures of the Mediterranean and Roman life. He returned to Rome in 1957 and has lived there ever since. Twombly's early work has a relationship to the sweeping expressionistic gestures of his Black Mountain associates but has developed with great freedom into a new intimate and personal language of thick paint smears, abstract marks, scrawls, graffiti, delicate lines, and vibration of light. He had his first show in New York in 1951 at the Kootz Gallery and has continued to exhibit regularly in major galleries worldwide ever since. Twombly has been the focus of numerous museum exhibitions including: Palais des Beaux-Arts, Brussels, in 1965, The Milwaukee Art Center in 1968, and several retrospective exhibitions—Bilder und Zeichnungen 1953–75, Munchen, Städtische Galerie im Lenbachhaus; *Cy Twombly Paintings and Drawings 1954–77,* the Whitney Museum of American Art; *Cy Twombly: Works on Paper 1957–87,* organized by Katherina Schmidt at the Staadtisches Kunstmuseum in Bonn and travelling to the Hamburg Museum and the Fundación Caja de Pensiones; and a major retrospective organized by Harold Szeeman for the Kunsthalle, Zurich, and travelling to the Whitechapel Art Gallery, London, Städtische Kunsthalle, Düsseldorf, Palacio de Velásquez, Madrid, and the Centre Georges Pompidou, Paris. Most recently he has exhibited his series, 15 Days at Illium, 1989-90, at the Philadelphia Museum of Art.

Gilbert & George: Gilbert was born in the Dolomites, Italy, in 1943; George, in Devon, England, in 1942. The two artists met in 1967 at the St. Martin's School of Art in London, where they were trained as sculptors. They began their lifetime commitment to collaborative work soon thereafter in 1968. Their first living sculpture performance, "Our New Sculpture (Underneath the Arches)," was presented at the St. Martin's School of Art in 1969, one year after their first exhibition at the London Gallery, Frank's Sandwich Bar. It was at this time that the two artists permanently collapsed the boundaries between their art and their lives with their manifesto, *The Laws of Sculptors,* which begins: "Always be smartly dressed, well groomed relaxed friendly polite and in complete control." Although the artists have always worked in a variety of media—photo-enlarged self-portrait grids, postcard collages, drawings, video, live performance and written art statements—the artists conceive of all their work as sculpture. The artists have been the subject of numerous museum exhibitions including solo-shows at the Whitechapel Art Gallery, London in 1971; the Stedelijk Museum, Amsterdam, in 1972; the Städtische Kunsthalle, Düsseldorf in 1981; and the Centre Georges Pompidou, Paris. A retrospective of the artists' work was organized by the Solomon R. Guggenheim Museum, New York, in 1985.

Francesco Clemente was born in Naples in 1952. His early academic interests centered around classical languages and literature, and he briefly enrolled as an architecture student at the University of Rome in 1970. Clemente first exhibited his work at the Galleria Valle Giulia in Rome in 1971, and continued to exhibit drawings, altered photographs and conceptual work throughout Europe in the 1970s. He made his first trip to India in 1973 and travelled through Afghanistan in 1974 with friend and fellow artist Alighiero Boetti. Clemente returned to India in 1977 and for a period of two years lived and worked in Madras, where he produced drawings, pastels, and his distinctive hand-made books. In 1980, he had his first exhibition in New York at Sperone Westwater Fischer gallery and was immediately recognized as an important member of the Italian Neo-Expressionist movement. Clemente, his wife, Alba, and their four children currently divide their time among New York, Rome, and Madras. Clemente's paintings, prints, and drawings—characterized by a detached symbolism and hieroglyphic, often sexually charged, narratives—have been the subject of numerous exhibitions travelling worldwide. These have included an exhibition of pastels organized by the Neue Nationalgalerie, Berlin, in 1984; an exhibition of paintings curated at the John and Mabel Ringling Museum of Art, Sarasota, in 1985; a drawings retrospective organized by the Museum fur Gegenwartskunst, Basel, in 1987; and an exhibition of prints curated at the

Milwaukee Art Museum in 1988. Clemente has collaborated with contemporary American poets, including John Wieners, Allen Ginsberg, Gregory Corso, Robert Creeley, and Rene Ricard. His illustrations to Alberto Savinio's *Departure of The Argonaut* were the subject of a travelling exhibition organized by the Museum of Modern Art, New York, in 1986. The artist's "Funerary Paintings" were exhibited at the Dia Art Foundation in New York in 1989, and a series of tapestries designed by Clemente and woven at El Taller Mexican de Gobelinos were exhibited at Mexico's Centro Cultural de Arte Contemporaneo in 1989–90.

Sigmar Polke was born in Oels (now Olesnica, Poland) in 1941 and moved, with his family, to West Germany at the age of 12. He attended the Kunstakademia in Dusseldorf from 1961–67 where he first met Joseph Beuys, Gerhard Hoeme, Blinky Palermo, and Gerhard Richter with whom he worked on a variety of painting and writing projects at that time. Throughout the 1970s and 1980s Polke travelled extensively, spending a great deal of time in Afghanistan, New Guinea, Australia, and Southeast Asia—areas the artist considers to be resonant with the seeds of primitive culture. During the 1970s Polke also made a series of 16mm films documenting the lives of his friends and acquaintances. Polke's paintings are a hybrid of photographic images and loosely worked abstraction, appropriating from all levels of culture—high, low, popular, domestic, and kitsch. His interest in Alchemy has led the artist to experiment with the use of a variety of resins and powdered materials to create translucent, tactile surfaces in his paintings. In fact, many of his works are dramatically altered by varying conditions of light, temperature, and humidity. He was the recipient of the Grand Prize at the São Paolo Bienal in 1975 and since then his work has been exhibited in gallery and museum exhibitions worldwide. Major exhibitions include one-man shows at the Städtische Kunsthalle, Düsseldorf in 1976; the Städtische Kunstmuseum, Bonn, in 1983; the Boysman-van Beuningen, Rotterdam, and Kunsthaus, Zurich, in 1984; and the Städtische Kunstmuseum, Bonn, in 1988. The artist currently lives and works in Cologne and Hamburg, where he has been a professor at the Hochschule fur Bildende Kunste since 1977.

Julian Schnabel was born in 1951 in New York. He moved with his family to Brownsville, Texas, in 1965 and studied at the University of Houston from 1969 to 1973. Schnabel attended the Whitney Museum of American Art Independent Study Program in New York from 1973 to 1974, after which he returned to Texas and exhibited his work at the

Contemporary Arts Museum, Houston. The artist returned to New York in 1976, and travelled extensively in Europe, visiting Paris, Milan, and Tuscany. He continued his European travels in 1978, visiting Italy, Germany and Spain, where he became interested in the architecture of Antoni Gaudí in Barcelona. At this time, Schnabel had his first European one-man show at the Galerie December in Düsseldorf. He exhibited his plate-paintings for the first time at Mary Boone Gallery, New York, in 1979 and began making sculpture in 1983. Schnabel has had one-man exhibitions at the Pace Gallery, New York, in 1984, 1986, and 1989. He was the subject of a major retrospective including work from 1975 to 1986 organized by the Whitechapel Art Gallery, London (travelling to the Centre Georges Pompidou, Paris; Städtische Kunsthalle, Düsseldorf; Whitney Museum of American Art, New York; San Francisco Museum of Modern Art; Museum of Fine Art, Houston). In 1988 "The Recognitions Paintings" were exhibited at the Cuartel del Carmen in Seville, Spain; the series was subsequently exhibited at the Kunsthalle, Basel, in 1989 in conjunction with the exhibition, "Arbeiten auf Papier 1975–1988" at the Museum fur Gegenwartkunst, Basel. In 1989, exhibitions of Schnabel's work were shown at the Musée d'Art Contemporain de Bordeaux and Museo d'Arte Contemporanea, Prato, Italy. The artist currently lives and works in New York City and Montauk.

Wolfgang Laib was born in Metzingen, West Germany, in 1950. While still a child, Laib moved with his family to India for several years and it was at that time that he first became interested in Buddhism. He enrolled in medical school in 1968 and upon completion of his dissertation on the purity of water, he became an M.D. in 1974. By 1975, however, he abandoned his scientific career in order to become an artist. His concern with meditation and purity—purity of form, purity of color and purity of materials—has informed his work since the earliest sculptures, The Milkstones—concave slabs of stone upon which fresh milk was poured daily. Art, for Laib, is a spiritual quest. His works seek to establish, for himself and for the viewer, a profound connection with nature. He continues to make minimal, site-specific works with materials such as pollen, rice, beeswax, and other organic substances. Major exhibitions include the Whitechapel Art Gallery, London, in 1985; the Musée d'Art Moderne de la Ville de Paris in 1986; and the Fundación Miró, Barcelona, in 1988. Laib currently lives and works on an organic farm in a small village in southern Germany and continues to make periodic trips to India.

Acknowledgments

I would like to thank

Louise Bourgeois
James Turrell
Enzo Cucchi
Vito Acconci
Cy Twombly
Gilbert & George
Francesco Clemente
Sigmar Polke
Julian Schnabel
Wolfgang Laib

for their openness and generosity,
without which this book could never have been done.

Thanks for the long and patient (!) collaboration to Alastair Thain and thanks also to Jill Wood and Richard Burbridge. In addition I would like to thank for their help and support Judy Adams, Bice Curiger, Raymond Foye, Don Kennison, Karen Marta, Paul Rickert, George Scrivani, Jean Silverthorne, Kim Spurlock, Helen Van der Meig, and Nigel Wingrove.